RELIGION FOR TODAY

Book Two

What Difference Does Religion Make?

CHRIS WRIGHT

OXFORD
UNIVERSITY PRESS

OXFORD
UNIVERSITY PRESS

Great Clarendon Street, Oxford OX2 6DP

Oxford University Press is a department of the University of Oxford. It furthers the University's objective of excellence in research, scholarship, and education by publishing worldwide in

Oxford New York

Auckland Bangkok Buenos Aires Cape Town Chennai Dar es Salaam Delhi Hong Kong Istanbul Karachi Kolkata Kuala Lumpur Madrid Melbourne Mexico City Mumbai Nairobi São Paulo Shanghai Taipei Tokyo Toronto

Oxford is a registered trade mark of Oxford University Press in the UK and in certain other countries

British Library Cataloguing in Publication Data

Data available

ISBN 0 19 914824 4

10 9 8 7 6 5 4 3 2 1

Typesetting and design: Carole Binding, Ruth Nason

Illustrations: Jason Brown, www.tranquildreams.com

Printed in Spain by Edelvives, Zaragoza

The Author and Publisher are grateful to the following for helpful comments at various times during the preparation of the book:

Leon Bernstein, Mark Brimicombe, Rasamandala Das, Roy Ahmad Jackson, Venerable Kusalo, Chris Prescott, Kanwaljit Kaur Singh, Jos Sumner

Cover photo: Clergy members baptise worshippers in a river near Newelton, Louisiana (Philip Gould/CORBIS).

Introduction

We live in a world where there are people of many different religions. In many of our towns and cities Buddhists, Christians, and Hindus live alongside Muslims, Jews, and Sikhs. If you travel abroad, you will soon experience whole countries that have been shaped by religion.

The *Religion for Today* series gives you the skills and knowledge to understand people with beliefs different from your own. In learning about other religions you will also have the chance to think about your own life. So you will not only learn *about* the religions you study; you will also learn *from* the religions.

Each book is packed with sources. Some are quotations from the sacred books of the religions. Others come from people who practise the religions. As you read each source you need to ask yourself: Who wrote it? Why did they write it? What sort of writing is it? Is the source reliable? Is it authoritative? Is it biased or one-sided? Do you agree with what is being said in the source? Do sources in the same unit contradict each other?

What difference does religion make? explores the difference that religion makes to people's lives. First we look at what it means to 'be religious'. We see how Buddhism began and how the Buddha's teachings affect people's lives today. We also study the life of Jesus. How has Jesus changed people's lives? In Units 3, 4, and 5 we think about specifically religious practices, such as going on pilgrimage to sacred places, reading sacred books, prayer, and celebrating stages in life with special ceremonies.

Contents

What difference does religion make?

More than three-quarters of the world's people consider that they belong to a religion. Where do religious feelings come from, and what difference does it make to people to be religious? We will begin to consider these questions in Unit 1.1. In Unit 1.2 we will look at how one particular religion, Buddhism, began and think about the influence that Buddhist beliefs may have on people's lives. The second part of this book concentrates on special religious practices, such as pilgrimage and prayer, but religious beliefs also influence what people do in all areas of their lives. Unit 1.3 looks at how religious beliefs have inspired people to actions which have changed the course of history.

▲ *What difference do you think religion makes to the lives of these people, who are talking after a service in a church in London? Do you think the care and concern that a priest, or other religious leader, gives is different from the care and concern shown by a non-religious person? If so, how?*

1.1

Being religious

From the earliest days of humankind it seems that some people have had a sense that there is more to life than the people and objects around them. Sometimes this is called having a sense of 'otherness', or a sense of the spiritual. Anyone who experiences this sense can be said to be 'being religious'.

How or why would such feelings have first occurred, for the first humans? People must sometimes have felt a sense of 'otherness' when faced with the forces of nature or the power of evil. Sometimes they must have wondered whether there might be a life after death. Sometimes they would just wonder why there was anything at all, and why they had an existence.

1 a Think of someone you think is religious. What makes you think they are religious?

b Do you think there is a difference between being religious and following a religion?

Sometimes – but not always – they explained the existence of life in terms of supernatural forces, and sometimes they believed in gods and goddesses. Some believed in just one God, as a creator and sustainer of the whole universe.

It seems that people shared these feelings with each other, wanted to understand them better, and gave them a special meaning. Some people became religious teachers and leaders, and their followers developed into groups with particular beliefs and customs. This would be how religions developed. 'Being religious' then took on another meaning: a religious person, as well as having religious feelings, is someone who follows the beliefs and practices of a religion.

Whom do we follow?

Throughout this book we will be looking at examples from six of the world's religions. In order of their beginning, they are: Hinduism, Judaism, Buddhism, Christianity, Islam, and Sikhism. Hinduism, Buddhism, and Sikhism developed in India, and Judaism, Christianity, and Islam developed in the Middle East. Some things about the religions are quite similar and some are very different. One way in which Buddhism and Christianity are similar is that both began with people following the vision of a particular religious teacher. Buddhists follow the Buddha's ideas about the meaning and purpose of life, which we will look at in Unit 1.2. Christians believe in the vision of Jesus, whose life and teaching we will study in Unit 2.

Making things sacred

All the religions we are studying have places that are special to them, perhaps because they are associated with where the religion began or because they make people feel particularly aware of the 'otherness' or religious side of life. Also, all the religions have developed ceremonies or customs to mark important times on the calendar and important occasions in a person's life, such as becoming an adult and getting married. Places and times and objects that are special in a religious way are called 'sacred', which means 'set apart (from normal everyday life) for religious use' or 'set apart for God'. In Units 3, 4, and 5 you will find out about sacred places, sacred books, and the way in which different religions make certain times and occasions sacred.

Hinduism has no founder. The origins of the religion are traced to a great civilisation living in the Indus Valley.

The origins of Judaism are traced to Abraham, 'father of the Jews', about 2000 BCE.

Buddhism began when Siddattha Gotama became enlightened, c.598 BCE, in India.

Christianity started as people followed the teachings of Jesus who was born into a Jewish family in present-day Israel in about 6 BCE.

Muslims say that their religion, Islam, is as old as humanity but that the Prophet Muhammad started the Islamic community in Arabia in 622 CE.

Sikhism was founded in 1499 by Guru Nanak, in the Punjab region of northern India.

What difference does it make?

Not everyone believes that there is a spiritual, religious side to life. Some people believe that this world is all there is [A]. What do you think? At the end of this unit (pages 10-11) we will consider why some people are religious and others not.

Throughout the book, the main question we are exploring is: What difference does religion make? How does it colour believers' lives? How does it influence the way they see the world and their ideas about the purpose of life? How does it affect what they do? So let's begin by taking a closer look at what 'being religious' means to some people.

source A

'Humanists think that this world and this life are all we have. Humanists reject the idea of any supernatural agency intervening to help or hinder us.'
British Humanist Association

> **2** Do you think that people who practise a religion are different from people who don't? Do you think they should be? In what ways?

Being religious means:

● **believing in a spiritual dimension**
Religious people believe that there is more to life than material existence. Each person has a spirit or soul. Many, though not all, religious people believe in a God who guides the world [B].

● **paying attention to the spiritual dimension through prayer or meditation**
For religious people who believe in a God, prayer is a way of communicating with him. In prayer, people seek God's guidance and help, and give praise and thanks. (We will look at prayer in more detail in Unit 4.)
Meditation means focusing your mind, in order to reach greater spiritual understanding.

source B

'I have always thought of my life as an open book. As Psalm 139 puts it: "O Lord you have searched me and know me. You perceive my thoughts. You are familiar with all my ways." Where God is concerned, there is no privacy at all. It's an odd kind of relationship. In one sense, it's a bit like being under the perpetual scrutiny of a security camera. It makes you think twice about what you do and think – which is probably no bad thing. But also it means, as Jesus told us, "Your Father knows what things you need before you ask him." And that can be good ... As regards God knowing everything about me, I've got used to it. Even if he were to offer to "respect my privacy", I don't know that I would take him up on it. After all, why would I want to hide anything from him? He's prepared to accept me as I am.'
BBC *Thought for the Day*, 23 February 2002, Professor Russell Stannard

◄ *A Muslim explains: '... when I stand for prayer ... I express whatever my needs are, my griefs are, my desires are ... I ask for forgiveness, I ask for a straight path, and I also ask for blessings in this world and in the hereafter ...'*

making life holy

Many religions teach that all that we have comes from God and will return to God. Followers of these religions believe that they should look after God's gifts and lift life up to God, to make it holy. Like the word 'sacred', 'holy' means 'set apart for God'.

Judaism describes religion as a task. The task is to raise ordinary life to a different level, and to make it holy. The Jewish holy book, the Bible, calls Jews to be a 'holy people'. It provides guidance on how to make life holy, by setting things apart for God. For example, one day a week, on the Shabbat, Jews set a day aside for God [C].

➤ *In Jewish homes each Friday evening, women draw in the light of the Shabbat candles.*

source C

'When the sun sets on Friday evening, I and millions of others leave this world. The worries of the week, or work, and of the world disappear for an entire day. If you entered my or most any home while celebrating Shabbat, you would be struck by the carefree and peaceful atmosphere, by the sense that none of us had anything troubling on our minds, and there seemed to be unlimited time for everyone in the home to devote to everyone else in the home.'

Denis Prager, 'Out of this World' in *Olam Magazine*, special issue on the Shabbat

seeing a meaning in life

Some people say that life has no meaning or purpose. You are born, grow old, and die, and that's it. But people's religious beliefs lead them to feel that there is more to life than that [D, E].

source D

'The end of life is not to be happy. The end of life is not to achieve pleasure and avoid pain. The end of life is to do the will of God, come what may.'

Martin Luther King Jr, *Paul's Letter to American Christians*, 4 November 1956

3 What does source C tell you about holiness?

4 a What do you think it means to say that religion is a task?

   b In what sense do Jews 'leave this world' on Friday evening? Do you think it is important to have a special holy day?

source E

'What we are here for ... is to work in such a way that the soul merges with the Supreme Soul. And this can only be achieved through prayer and devoting your time that way.'

Harbans Singh Sagoo, quoted in J. Bowker, *Worlds of Faith*

Many religions teach that our present life is a prelude to a more important life beyond, and that the way we live now has eternal consequences.

Belief in an afterlife can provide a reason for people to be moral in this life. Hindus and Sikhs believe that the soul is re-embodied after death, and that the way a person lives now determines the condition in which the soul will be reborn. Christians and Muslims believe in an eternal life after death, and that a person's behaviour on earth affects what happens to them in that eternal life.

source F

'If it could be proved that there is NO life after death, then a great many people would certainly give up bothering to be religious – there would be no happy reward or reunion to come, so no longer any point in trying.'

Rosalyn Kendrick, *The Trouble with God*

5 a Complete the following sentence for yourself:
   I believe that the purpose of life is …

   b Do you think you are going to fulfil this purpose? What steps are you taking to fulfil it?

● **having one's attitudes challenged**

All great religious teachers have used spiritual stories to instruct and guide people. The stories challenge people's attitudes, beliefs, and values. Anthony de Mello was a spiritual teacher who lived in India. He drew on the spiritual traditions of many countries, cultures, and religions. He often used the title 'Master' to describe a religious teacher. What do you think his stories in sources G and H are trying to teach? What changes are they trying to bring about in people's lives?

▲ *Belief in an afterlife can have tragic consequences. Belief that they will be rewarded with a place in Paradise is one factor that motivates young Muslims, like this woman's son, to become suicide bombers in the conflict between Palestinians and Israel.*

source G

Dreams

'When will I be Enlightened?'

'When you see,' the Master said.

'See what?'

'Trees and flowers and moon and stars.'

'But I see these every day.'

'No. What you see is paper trees, paper flowers, paper moons and paper stars. For you live not in reality but in your words and thoughts.'

And for good reason, he added gently, 'You live a paper life alas, and you will die a paper death.'

A. de Mello, *One Minute Wisdom*

Happiness

'I am in desperate need of help – or I'll go crazy. We're living in a single room – my wife, my children and my in-laws. So our nerves are on edge, we yell and scream at one another. The room is a hell.'

'Do you promise to do whatever I tell you?' said the Master gravely.

'I swear I shall do anything.'

'Very well. How many animals do you have?'

'A cow, a goat and six chickens.'

'Take them all into the room with you. Then come back after a week.'

The disciple was appalled. But he had promised to obey! So he took the animals in. A week later he came back, a pitiable figure, moaning, 'I'm a nervous wreck. The dirt! The stench! The noise! We're all on the verge of madness!'

'Go back,' said the Master, 'and put the animals out.'

The man ran all the way home. And came back the following day, his eyes sparkling with joy. 'How sweet life is! The animals are out. The home is a Paradise – so quiet and clean and roomy!'

A. de Mello, *One Minute Wisdom*

6 It has been said that 'the shortest distance between a human being and the Truth is a story'. Why do you think so many religious teachers use stories?

● standing up for your beliefs

Standing up for what you believe, and being an ambassador for your religion, can be costly. Throughout history and in many places around the world today, people suffer different forms of persecution because of their religion. There is also a dark side to religion, in that religious beliefs sometimes breed violence and hatred.

▼ *More Christians died for their faith in the twentieth century than in the previous nineteen centuries combined and many others suffered other kinds of persecution. Here, Christians protesting against religious discrimination in Pakistan are chased by police.*

7 Why do you think religion is so often at the centre of violence, as well as at the centre of the struggle for peace?

Is there a spiritual dimension? Why are some people religious and others not?

8 In pairs, write down your thoughts under these headings:

a Evidence that there IS a spiritual dimension to life

b Evidence that there IS NOT a spiritual dimension

9 'I would believe in a spiritual dimension in life if it could be proved.' What do you think the word 'proved' means in this context? What would count as proof?

Philosophers have put forward ideas about whether there is really a spiritual, 'otherness', dimension to life. One German philosopher, Ludwig Feuerbach (1804-72) argued that what people call God is the result of their needs and wishes. He taught that people have a need to believe in a God who is there to guide and help them. They also have a need to believe that death is not the end – that there is an afterlife. Therefore, people have created a God in their own imagination. They have given God a personality they can trust – intelligent, good, and loving.

Blaise Pascal (1623-62) was a French philosopher, mathematician, and physicist. He argued that God's existence can neither be proved nor disproved. But each person has to make a gamble and choose whether God exists or not. You cannot live in this world without making your choice. Pascal said that it is worth gambling that God does exist, because, if you gamble that God doesn't exist and He actually does, you will lose out on the benefits that belief in God can bring – in this life and in the afterlife. And if you gamble that God doesn't exist and you are correct, you will have gained nothing.

In sources J, K, L, and M, some ordinary people from today talk about why they have or have not chosen to believe in God and to follow a religion.

source J

'I believe in God not because I can prove God's existence with my mind but because the evidence makes his existence probable. I have made the decision to trust God with my life. My life is an act of faith.'

Mary

10 What is the imagination? What do you imagine? Does what you imagine exist?

11 Do you think that Feuerbach managed to prove that God does not exist? What are the strengths and the weaknesses of his argument?

12 a Explain what Pascal meant when he said that making a decision about God's existence is a gamble.

b Religious people say they have faith. What do you think is the difference between gambling that God exists and having faith that God exists?

13 What do sources J, K, L, and M tell you about why some people are religious and others not?

14 How much does a person's upbringing influence whether they are religious or not?

15 What aspects of religion do you find (a) attractive and (b) off-putting? Explain your answer.

'I was born into a religious family. Ever since I was a baby my parents took me to the Temple. In our house we have a shrine at which we make offerings each day. Being religious is an essential part of who I am.'

Nisha

◄ *Why do you think that, for some people, shafts of light give a feeling of the spiritual dimension?*

'If there were truly a god, then he must be a most cruel one to allow the horrible things that man does to his fellow man. To call the villains of our society "animals" does the animal injustice. Most animals are not cruel to one another – they kill one another for food or to protect themselves and their young, but they do not kill for the sheer "joy" of killing. I do not believe that man is created in the image of god, but that god is created in the image of man.'

Martha Stanard,
www.positiveatheism.org/mail

'Growing up in a ... non-religious family, I never heard the name of God being uttered, I never saw anyone pray and I learned early on that the only reason for doing things was to benefit yourself. I went through high school with a breeze. I felt that nothing could harm me ...

In college I started thinking about the meaning of life. I had a hard time accepting any religion because of all the wars and problems relating to them. I made up my own philosophy. I was convinced that some form of power created everything but I couldn't say it was God.

I believed in a life after death because I just couldn't believe that justice wouldn't be served. I also believed that everything happens for a reason.

In my last year of college ... I started asking questions and reading books, but most importantly, I started socialising with Muslims ... The Muslims that I met were wonderful people. They accepted me right away and they never forced anything on me. They were more generous to me than my own family. Islam seemed to be a good system of life and I acknowledged the structure and stability it provided but I was not convinced it was for me.

I had a period of brain storming when I was thinking over all the new things I learnt. I felt my heart softening and I tried to imagine life as a Muslim. I saw a humble life full of honesty, generosity, stability, peace, respect and kindness. Most of all I saw a life with a MEANING.

I knew I had to let go of my ego and humble myself before something much more powerful than myself.'

www.usc.edu/dept/MSA/newmuslims/helena

16 What difference does religion make? In your answer, consider the following:
- how does someone who is not religious view life? You may like to find out more about humanist beliefs, from www.humanism.org.uk
- what does a religious person think about (a) the spiritual dimension, (b) the purpose of life, and (c) communication with God?

What difference has the Buddha made?

The story of Siddattha Gotama

Siddattha Gotama (who became the Buddha) was born about 563 BCE in a village called Lumbini, in India. His parents lived in a splendid palace. His father ruled the Shakya tribe.

There are many legends about Siddattha's birth. One tells that his mother, the queen, had a dream that a white elephant with six tusks pierced her womb. Ten months later, on her way to her father's house in Lumbini, she asked the carriage to stop in a beautiful moonlit grove. As she walked through the grove she felt great pain. She gave birth to Siddattha Gotama while she was resting.

The baby was taken to the palace, where a wise man called Asita came to visit him. He told the parents: 'This boy will be a king of kings, or a great holy man.'

Asita's prophecy worried the king. He wanted Siddattha to be king of kings, but he knew that some things, such as the sight of suffering, were likely to drive him to become a holy man. Therefore the king tried to keep his son away from suffering. He arranged for Siddattha to marry a beautiful princess and gave him all the comforts of life. Soon a son was born to the young couple. 'Good!' the king thought. 'Now Siddattha will never think of becoming a holy man.'

Siddattha became curious about life outside the palace. When he was 29, he took a chariot ride through the city. His father ordered all unhappy sights to be kept away from him. However, Siddattha saw three things that disturbed him: an old man, a sick man, and a dead man. He had not known that old age, sickness, and death were part of life. Then he saw a fourth sight. 'Stop! Who is that? He looks calm and different from the other men I have seen.' The charioteer replied, 'He is a holy man who has given up a life of pleasure and pain in search of truth.'

In the middle of the night Siddattha decided: 'I must find a way to end sorrow. I will go in search of truth, like that holy man.' He left the palace – his wife and his child – and went into the forest. He changed his rich robes and jewellery for the clothes of a beggar.

Siddattha went in search of the Hindu holy men. He had discovered that riches did not make him happy, so he tried their way. Like them, he denied himself all luxuries and tried to live on little food. He came to look like a skeleton. One day he collapsed and realised that this could not be the way to end unhappiness. The human body could not escape disease, old age, and death.

Siddattha sat to meditate under a bodhi tree. He was determined not to move away until he had found the way to end unhappiness. Visions of his old luxurious life in the palace floated before his eyes, but nothing could tempt him away. Then, for the first time, he understood the world as it really was. 'I know the truth now. The way to end sorrow is found.' This event in Siddattha's life is known as his 'Enlightenment'. He became known as the Buddha, which means 'the enlightened one'.

The Buddha was 35 when he became enlightened. For the next 45 years he travelled around northern India teaching others about his understanding of the truth about the world. He taught about a way to end sorrow: a 'Middle Way' between having everything and having nothing. His teaching inspired many others and soon Buddhism spread throughout Asia.

The Buddha's teaching

As he meditated under the bodhi tree, the Buddha reached Enlightenment. This is a state of perfect understanding of the way life is, its meaning, and purpose. Buddhists believe that, by following the teachings and practices of their religion, they too may reach that state of Enlightenment. That is their ultimate aim.

In his teaching, the Buddha tried to tell people what he had understood about why there is suffering and how it can be ended. He taught that all things change, and that the reason why we are never lastingly happy is that we cling to things, such as material possessions and human emotions, which will always change and fade. The way to end unhappiness and suffering is to stop clinging to things [A, B, C].

The Buddha taught that there is an 'Eightfold Path' to the end of suffering and to Enlightenment. This path is represented by the eight-spoked *Dhamma* wheel. *Dhamma* means 'the law of life'.

◄ *The Eightfold Path has eight areas in which Buddhists try to develop. Right Understanding and Right Intention are to do with developing wisdom. Right Speech, Right Action, and Right Livelihood are to do with moral behaviour. Right Effort, Right Awareness, and Right Concentration are to do with training the mind and thoughts.*

The *Dhammapada* is one of the most famous collections of Buddhist scriptures. It contains teachings of the Buddha, like those shown in sources A-F.

source D

'Hatred is never appeased by hatred in this world; by non-hatred alone is hatred appeased.'

Dhammapada 5

source E

'Though one may conquer a thousand times a thousand men in battle, yet he indeed is the noblest victor who conquers himself.'

Dhammapada 103

source F

'Like a beautiful flower full of colour and also fragrant, even so, fruitful are the fair words of one who practises them. As from a great heap of flowers many garlands can be made, even so should many good deeds be done by one born a mortal.'

Dhammapada 52-53

◄ *The first stage of meditation is to let the mind become completely calm, untroubled by busy thoughts. The next stage is noticing the thoughts and emotions that arise from the mind, but without being distracted by them and letting them disturb the calm. The aim of meditation for Buddhists is to see the truth about the way things are.*

source G

'Now the Buddha himself went through six years of self-mortification; he suffered for six years. And then previous to that he had been the son of a Prince and had lived a rich, comfortable life. So he's had the two extremes, and he says that both extremes are wrong, and that the only correct way is the Middle Way. So because he has gone through all the range of experience I can trust him myself.'

Mr Wickramaratne, quoted in J. Bowker, *Worlds of Faith*

1 One part of the Eightfold Path is 'Right Speech'. Try to live out the Buddha's teaching on this for a week, by saying only helpful things to people and never saying anything hurtful. Keep a daily record of things you said and how easy or difficult the task is.

2 The Eightfold Path is called a 'Middle Way' to Enlightenment. Read source G and explain what it means to live according to the Middle Way. Think of examples to show how Buddhists could follow the Middle Way in everyday life today.

Finding Nirvana

Buddhism began in India and grew out of Hinduism. Buddhists, like Hindus, believe that all living things are caught up in a cycle of birth, death, and rebirth, called *samsara*. When a living creature dies, the soul that entered it at its birth is reborn in a new living creature. Like Hindus, Buddhists also believe that it is possible to escape from this cycle.

Buddhists believe that they are released from the cycle of *samsara* when they reach Enlightenment. They then enter a state of eternal peace and contentment called *Nirvana*. *Nirvana* is sometimes described as the blowing out of the flames of hatred, greed, and ignorance. These flames are said to fuel the cycle of *samsara*.

The Buddha had a vision that all people would become enlightened and find the peace of *Nirvana*. *Nirvana* is a Sanskrit word. Some Buddhist scriptures were written in this Indian language and others were written in Pali. In Pali, *Nirvana* is called *Nibbana*. Source H shows how a Buddhist monk called Nagasena explained *Nibbana* in the second century BCE.

> **3** How does Nagasena try to describe Nibbana to King Milinda? Try drawing your own picture to represent Nibbana.

source H

Nagasena answers King Milinda's questions

'Great king, just as, although the great ocean exists, it is impossible to measure the water or count the living beings that make their abode there, precisely so, great king, although Nibbana really exists, it is impossible to make clear the form or figure or age or dimensions of Nibbana.

Just as the lotus is not polluted by water, so also Nibbana is not polluted by any of the Depravities …

Just as water is cool and quenches fever, so also Nibbana is cool and quenches every one of the Depravities.

But again further, medicine puts an end to bodily ills. Precisely so Nibbana puts an end to all sufferings …

Just as food is the support of life of all human beings, so also Nibbana, once realised, is the support of life, for it destroys old age and death …

Just as a mountain-peak is exceedingly lofty, so also Nibbana is exceedingly lofty.'

The Milindapanha from *The World of the Buddha*, edited by L. Stryk

Theravada and Mahayana

In the centuries after the death of the Buddha, Buddhism developed into a variety of streams. The name *Mahayana*, which means 'great vehicle' or 'great way', was given to a whole group of these. They claimed to offer more ways to Enlightenment than other types of Buddhism. Today, Mahayana Buddhism is practised widely in Tibet, China, and Japan.

The other main strand of Buddhism today is *Theravada* Buddhism. It is the only surviving school of Buddhism from before Mahayana. A basic idea of Theravada is that the only way to reach Enlightenment is to follow the example and teachings of the Buddha. Theravada Buddhism is practised widely in Thailand, Burma, Sri Lanka, and Cambodia.

The way of the bodhisattva

A central teaching of Mahayana Buddhism is about the way of the *bodhisattva*. A *bodhisattva* is an enlightened being who chooses not to enter *Nirvana* but to stay in this world to help others reach Enlightenment. The *bodhisattva*'s aim is to lead all beings to *Nirvana*.

In one sacred text the *bodhisattva* is compared to a brave hero who finds himself in a forest of terrors with his family. Instead of abandoning his family in order to run for safety himself, he stays with them to reassure them and uses all his powers to defeat the terrors and bring everyone safely home. *Bodhisattvas* are wise and so compassionate that they put the happiness of all beings in the universe above their own.

Mahayana Buddhism envisages a future where more and more beings dedicate their lives to the enlightenment of all, helping more people to make spiritual progress and so developing more wisdom and compassion in the world.

➤ *The bodhisattva Avalokiteshvara is often pictured with thousands of arms, ready to help everyone at once. Tibetan Buddhists believe that Avalokiteshvara works through their religious leader, the Dalai Lama (above). They believe the Dalai Lama is an earthly instrument of the bodhisattva, showing wisdom and compassion.*

How do religious beliefs influence actions?

We are going to look at how the beliefs of two famous people inspired them to act in a way that changed the course of history. The first, Mahatma Gandhi (1869-1948), was brought up as a Hindu. He became the leader of the Indian nationalist movement which sought to make India independent from British colonial rule. He built on the Hindu belief in non-violence, called *ahimsa*, to develop a new method of non-violent resistance, which he called *satyagraha*. Through his efforts, India was granted independence.

The story of Mahatma Gandhi

Mahatma Gandhi – Key beliefs

Gandhi's teachings and actions were based on the following Hindu ideas, although he was also influenced by Western thought and Christianity:

- God is in everything. God is the central quality of all objects.

- All people have God in them and are therefore equal, spiritually. Love is the only appropriate relationship between people, shown in selfless action for the sake of others.

- Non-violence (*ahimsa*) is taught in the Hindu Laws of Manu, which say: 'Let him bless when he is cursed.'

Mohandas Karamchand Gandhi was born into a merchant family in India on 2 October 1869.

When he was 19, he travelled to England to study Law. He enjoyed England, but was shunned by his fellow students because he was Indian. In London he read a book called *Civil Disobedience* by Henry Thoreau. This introduced him to the idea of non-violent resistance.

Two years later, in 1893, he left India to practise law in South Africa. He was deeply troubled by the racism he experienced against Indians. He stayed in South Africa for 20 years, fighting injustice. He developed the idea of peaceful protests and went to jail twice for his acts of civil disobedience.

In 1914 Gandhi returned to India, which was ruled by the British. As leader of the Indian National Congress Party, he campaigned for home rule and independence from British rule. In 1920 Gandhi urged Indians to boycott British courts and government and to make their own fabrics in order to replace goods from Britain. This led to his imprisonment in 1922-24.

The British rulers levied a tax on salt. So in 1930 Gandhi led thousands of Indians on a 200-mile march to the Indian Ocean to make their own salt. Again he was jailed. In 1935 he said: 'In my opinion non-violence is not passivity ... Non-violence, as I understand it, is the most active force in the world ... Non-violence is the supreme law. During my half a century of experience I have not yet come across a situation when I had to say that I was helpless, that I had no remedy in terms of non-violence.'

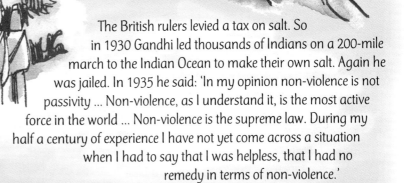

Gandhi was convinced that India would never be totally free until it ruled itself. At the beginning of the Second World War he demanded independence for India in return for India helping Britain during the war. India finally gained independence in 1947.

India had gained independence, but it was at the cost of the violent partitioning of the country into India and Pakistan. Nearly one million people died in riots between Hindus and Muslims. When Gandhi saw this, he again turned to non-violent protest. He went on hunger strike, saying that he would not eat until the violence stopped.

Gandhi's attempts to bring about reconciliation between Hindus and Muslims resulted in his own death. A fellow Hindu, who felt that Gandhi had betrayed the Hindu cause, assassinated him on 30 January 1948. He shot Gandhi three times in the chest, as he was making his way to a prayer meeting.

Martin Luther King

Gandhi's ideas inspired non-violent activism in many parts of the world – including in the USA, where Martin Luther King Jr (1929-68), the son of a Christian minister, became one of the main leaders of the civil rights movement.

The story of Martin Luther King

Martin Luther King was born on 15 January 1929, in Atlanta, Georgia. His father was a Baptist minister and named his son after a sixteenth-century German religious reformer, Martin Luther. When Martin was five, he played games with white boys until their mother told them that they could not play with him because he was black.

Martin Luther King – Key beliefs

● God made the world and all things in it [Genesis 1: 26]. People are called to obey God's standards and stand up for the truth of God.

● All people are precious to God, since they are made in God's image [Genesis 1], and there should be no distinction between people [Galatians 3: 28].

● We are called to love and serve each other, as God loves us [1 John 4: 7-12].

● God is a God of justice, who calls his people to act against injustice in the world.

● Jesus commands his disciples to love their enemies [Matthew 5: 44], so Christians should fight injustice with the weapons of love, rather than violence. Love has the power to change the world. This may be costly [Matthew 5: 10].

Racial discrimination was a great problem in America in the 1950s and 1960s. Black people were treated as second-class citizens. Segregation laws said that they had to sit at the back of buses, could not eat in restaurants with whites, and had to use separate schools, swimming pools, hotels, and so on. Martin Luther King suffered from this discrimination.

He decided to become a minister in the Baptist Church, like his father. In his studies he learned about Gandhi's non-violent leadership in India and was impressed by Gandhi's example.

On 1 December 1955 a black woman named Rosa Parks refused to give up her bus seat for a white man. She was arrested and taken to jail.

An association was formed to fight the segregation laws, using the case of Rosa Parks. Martin Luther King became its president. He organised a boycott of the city buses. The boycott was very successful and was the beginning of the fight for civil rights for blacks.

For the next 12 years King led the civil rights movement in the American South. He made speeches and led marches and other protests, all using non-violent means.

In his most famous speech about his dream of an equal society in America (page 23) he said: 'We must rise to the majestic heights of meeting physical force with soul force.' His leadership of the civil rights movement won him the Nobel Peace Prize in 1964.

Many people loved and respected King for his work, but others feared and hated him. His house and church were bombed and he was threatened and beaten. But none of this stopped him working in a non-violent way.

In a speech on 3 April 1968 he said: 'I've seen the Promised Land [of equality between blacks and whites in America]. I may not get there with you, but as a people we will get to the Promised Land.' The very next day he was assassinated in Memphis, Tennessee.

Some extracts from Gandhi's speeches

'Passive resistance is a method of securing rights by personal suffering; it is the reverse of resistance by arms … Jesus Christ, Daniel, and Socrates represented the purest form of passive resistance or soul force.'

'Non-violence succeeds only when we have a real living faith in God.'

'The golden rule is to act fearlessly upon what one believes to be right.'

'What is faith if it is not translated into action?'

'Non-cooperation with evil is as much a duty as cooperation with good.'

'My notion of democracy is that under it the weakest should have the same opportunity as the strongest.'

'Non violence is the first article of my faith. It is also the last article of my creed.'

1 **a** What do you learn about Gandhi's beliefs from the story on pages 18-19?

   b What did Gandhi mean when he spoke about non-violent resistance? What creative methods of non-violent resistance did Gandhi use? (See also the quotations on this page.)

   c Do you think these methods were effective?

2 Write a Charter for Non-Violence that people could use in settling disputes amongst themselves. In this charter, list all the possible methods of non-violence.

➤ *Christian boys hold symbols of Islam, Christianity, and Hinduism during a rally calling for an end to violence between Hindus and Muslims in Gujarat, India, in 2002. Behind them is a statue of Mahatma Gandhi.*

'I have a dream'

On 28 August 1963 Martin Luther King delivered this famous speech, calling all Americans to treat black people ('Negroes') justly and give them equal rights.

'Now is the time to rise from the dark and desolate valley of segregation to the sunlit path of racial justice. Now is the time to open the doors of opportunity to all of God's children ...

We can never be satisfied as long as a Negro in Mississippi cannot vote and a Negro in New York believes he has nothing for which to vote ... we will not be satisfied until justice rolls down like waters and righteousness like a mighty stream.

I say to you today, my friends, that in spite of the difficulties and frustrations of the moment, I still have a dream. It is a dream deeply rooted in the American dream.

I have a dream that one day this nation will rise up and live out the true meaning of its creed: "We hold these truths to be self-evident: that all men are created equal." I have a dream that one day on the red hills of Georgia the sons of former slaves and the sons of former slave owners will be able to sit down together at a table of brotherhood ... I have a dream that my four children will one day live in a nation where they will not be judged by the colour of their skin but by the content of their character. I have a dream today.

I have a dream that one day the state of Alabama ... will be transformed into a situation where little black boys and black girls will be able to join hands with little white boys and white girls and walk together as sisters and brothers. I have a dream today. This is our hope. This is the faith with which I return to the South. With this faith we will be able to hew out of the mountain of despair a stone of hope. With this faith we will be able to transform the jangling discords of our nation into a beautiful symphony of brotherhood. With this faith we will be able to work together, to pray together, to struggle together, to go to jail together, to stand up for freedom together, knowing that we will be free one day.

When we let freedom ring ... we will be able to speed up that day when all of God's children, black men and white men, Jews and Gentiles, Protestants and Catholics, will be able to join hands and sing in the words of the old Negro spiritual, "Free at last! free at last! thank God Almighty, we are free at last!"'

3 a Why did Martin Luther King deserve the Nobel Peace Prize?

b What do you think he was referring to when he spoke of the 'Promised Land' the evening before his death? (See page 21.)

4 Take each of the key beliefs from the box on page 20 and show how Martin Luther King lived out these beliefs. Find evidence from his life (pages 20-21) and from his 'I have a dream' speech.

What difference has Jesus made?

Jesus is a dominant figure in Western history and culture. Many of Western society's values and standards of behaviour are based on Jesus' teaching, even though people following these values and standards may not think they are religious at all. According to one estimate, an average of four books about Jesus are published every day. Today, the religion founded on the life and teaching of Jesus is the world's largest religion, with two billion followers. Why has Jesus had such an impact? In Unit 2 you will learn how his life and death have made a difference to so many people.

2.1

source A

The Emperor Napoleon said: 'Alexander, Caesar, Charlemagne, and I have built great empires. They depended on force. But long ago Jesus started an empire that depended on love, and even to this day millions will die for him.'

Why was Jesus born?

Across the world at midnight on 31 December 1999 people watched firework displays to celebrate the end of one millennium and the beginning of another. Millennium means a thousand years. In the year 2000 the Christian Church was celebrating the 2000th birthday of Jesus.

But, according to a survey published in the *Daily Telegraph*, only 1 per cent of 687 children between the ages of 7 and 11 connected the Millennium with Jesus. Most associated it with the Dome (16 per cent), the Millennium bug (9 per cent), and the hit song 'Millennium' by Robbie Williams (9 per cent). Such a survey suggests that many children do not understand the significance of Jesus' birth for Christians.

1 Brainstorm the word 'millennium'. What do you associate with the word? What events do you remember?

2 In groups, create your own Top Ten list of people who lived in the last millennium. What criteria will you use? Will you include the most influential, the most good, the worst, the most popular, ...?

24

Jesus the rescuer

Christianity is centred on Jesus, which is a Hebrew name meaning 'God rescues'. Christians believe that God sent Jesus into the world on a rescue mission to save humanity from sin and its consequences. This rescue mission cost Jesus his life.

Christians believe that human beings are in need of rescuing, rather like the yachtsman in source B. They believe that Jesus' rescue mission was predicted by prophets, whose words are recorded in the Hebrew Bible. This is the Bible of the Jewish people, and also the part of the Christian Bible known as the Old Testament.

➤ *Christians in California try to persuade others to believe in Jesus. What does this picture tell you about Christian beliefs about Jesus?*

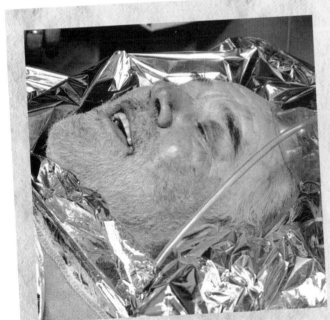

source B

Rescued!

Yachtsman Tony Bullimore was rescued yesterday, after the world had given him up for dead. He had spent most of four days huddling for warmth in a makeshift hammock inside his upturned yacht, after it capsized. Outside, the storm raged. The temperature fell to freezing. Bullimore's nightmare ended when he heard banging on the hull of the yacht and the voice of an Australian diver. Bullimore said: 'When I saw the ship there and the plane overhead and a couple of guys peering over the upturned hull, it was heaven, absolute heaven, I felt like a new man. I felt like I had been brought to life again.'
(10 January 1997)

3 What would you feel like if you were being rescued like Tony Bullimore [B]? Have you ever been caught in a situation when you needed rescuing?

4 People need rescuing in many different ways – sometimes from negative things they do to themselves. In small groups, explore what 'rescuing' means in the following situations, and how you would go about rescuing the person:
   – rescuing a friend from drugs
   – rescuing a friend from a destructive relationship (e.g. abuse at home, or a possessive boyfriend or girlfriend)

Hebrew prophecies

Sources C and D are words of the prophet Isaiah, who lived in the eighth century BCE. At this time the Jewish people, called 'the nation of Judah', were tempted to make military alliances with foreign powers in order to protect their nation. But Isaiah believed that Judah should rely on God. He also spoke out against the rich and powerful who neglected and oppressed the poor. He prophesied that the Jews would be punished for this, but that a small number of them would be rescued. They would then live in a perfect age, ruled by a righteous descendant of King David. This righteous ruler, chosen by God, was called the Messiah.

Jewish people do not believe that Isaiah's prophecies have been fulfilled, but Christians believe that they have come true. Christians believe that Jesus was the promised Messiah. The Greek word for Messiah is 'Christos', and this is why Christians often refer to their rescuer as Jesus Christ.

5 What did Isaiah tell the Jews the Messiah would be like [C, D]?

6 How important is the concept of rescue to Christians?

What happened at Jesus' birth?

Accounts of Jesus' birth are found in the New Testament of the Christian Bible. This includes four books that relate the life of Jesus. They are known as the Gospels, which means 'good news'. Two of the Gospels, Matthew and Luke, tell the story of Jesus' birth in a stable in Bethlehem [E]. Luke describes how shepherds visited the baby Jesus, and Matthew records that wise men from the East came to see him. The Gospel of John does not tell the birth story, but begins with a poem about the meaning of Jesus' birth [F]. It describes the central Christian belief that God became a human person in Jesus.

In 'The Creche' (1929-33) by the Italian-American painter Joseph Stella, the shepherds of Bethlehem and the wise men from the East stand for 'all tribes and peoples and tongues' (Revelation 7: 9) as well as for all social and economic classes, united in the worship of the child Jesus.

> Christians celebrate the birth of Jesus in their Christmas festival.

source F

John's poem

'Before the world was created,
the Word already existed;
he was with God,
and he was the same as God …

Through him God made all things …
The Word was the source of life,
and this life brought light to mankind …

The Word became a human being and,
full of grace and truth,
lived among us.
We saw his glory,
the glory which he received as the Father's only Son.'

John 1: 1-14

7 How does John's account of Jesus' birth [F] differ from Luke's [E]? Which account appears more often on Christmas cards? Why do you think this is the case?

8 What do you learn about Jesus from John's account [F]? Design a Christmas card based on John 1: 1-14 to send to a Christian friend. What difficulties do you encounter? Why?

The meaning of Jesus' birth

Christians believe that Jesus is the Son of God, who lived on earth as a human. The word used for 'God becoming human' or 'God becoming flesh' in the person of Jesus is the 'Incarnation'. The Incarnation is a mystery that writers and artists have struggled to describe. For example, Sören Kierkegaard, a Danish philosopher, wrote a story of a king loving a humble maiden, to try to explain why Jesus was born [I]. Dorothy Sayers [G] expresses the idea that God became a human being in order to live alongside people, to understand their lives from the inside. Christians believe that Jesus understands all their sufferings [H].

'The Heavenly and Earthly Trinities', by Bartolome Esteban Murillo, 1681-82. 'Trinity' means three. The child Jesus is placed in the centre of the painting. How has Murillo shown Jesus to be both fully divine and fully human? Who makes up the earthly trinity? Who makes up the heavenly trinity?

'For whatever reason God chose to make man as he is – limited and suffering and subject to sorrows and death – He had the honesty and courage to take His own medicine. Whatever game He is playing with His creation, He has kept His own rules and played fair. He can exact nothing from man that He has not exacted from Himself. He has Himself gone through the whole of human experience, from the trivial irritations of family life and the cramping restrictions of hard work and lack of money to the worst horrors of pain and humiliation, defeat, despair, and death. When He was a man, He played the man. He was born in poverty and died in disgrace and thought it well worthwhile.'

Dorothy Sayers, *Christian Letters To a Post-Christian World*

9 **a** What is the point being made in source G?

b Make a list of what the source says about the nature of God (e.g.,God is fair).

c The source refers to the difficulties of human life, but not the joys. Make a list of the joys of being human. If you were to create a picture of Jesus experiencing the joys of human life, how would you show him? Draw a sketch and give it a caption.

'For we do not have a high priest who is unable to sympathise with our weaknesses, but we have one who has been tempted in every way.'

Hebrews 4: 15

Kierkegaard's Parable

Once there was a king
Who loved a humble maiden.
This king was so powerful and well established
That he could not marry her
Without being forced to abdicate.
If he was to marry her,
The king knew that he would make her forever grateful.

It occurred to him, though,
That something would be wanting in her happiness.
She would always admire him and thank him,
But she would not be able to love him
For the inequality between them would be too great,
And she would never be able to forget
Her humble origin and her debt of gratitude.

So he decided upon another way.
Instead of making her queen,
He would renounce the kingship.
He would become a commoner
And then offer her his love.
In doing this he realised that he was taking a great risk,
He was doing something that would be foolish
In the eyes of most people in his kingdom,
Perhaps even in her eyes.
He would lose the kingship,
And he might also be rejected by her
Especially if she were disappointed at not becoming queen.

Yet he decided to take this risk.
It was better, he believed, to risk everything
In order to make love possible.

10 a In source I, why couldn't the king marry the maiden and remain king? Why did the king become a commoner? Why was this a risk?

b What do you learn from sources G and I about Christian beliefs about the sacrifice God/Jesus made in becoming human, the suffering that Jesus would have to endure on earth, and the human experiences he would have to share?

2.2

Was Jesus a revolutionary?

A revolution often means a successful attempt by a large group of people to completely change the way their country is governed. Usually, force is used to overthrow the old rulers. In History, you learn about the French Revolution and the Russian Revolution. A revolutionary is someone who takes part in a revolution or someone who argues for a fundamental change to the way that a country or an organisation is run. Some people see Jesus as a revolutionary, whose ideas encouraged people to rebel against their religious and political leaders. This explains why the Jewish religious authorities and the Roman political authorities disliked Jesus and sought to bring about his death [A]. In this unit you will learn why the authorities considered Jesus to be dangerous and how he brought about a revolution in people's values and beliefs.

▲ *A Chinese picture of Jesus. Why might a government be worried by such a picture?*

◄ *In the time of Jesus, different parts of Palestine had different Roman rulers.*

Decapolis, a federation of 10 cities

Subject to Pontius Pilate

Subject to Herod Antipas

Mediterranean Sea

Capernaum
Cana
GALILEE
Nazareth
Nain

DECAPOLIS

SAMARIA

River Jordan

PEREA

Emmaus

Jerusalem   Bethany
Bethlehem

JUDEA

IDUMAEA

source A

'Jesus was declaring a whole new way of life based on a picture of reality which, curiously enough, threatened many of his own people's traditions and the rule of Rome at the same time: no small feat! A young rebel, Jesus was not afraid to upset traditional apple carts and precipitate popularly perceived scandals by his own unconventional actions. Jesus was put to death through the collusion of the Roman governor, Pilate the Procurator of Judea, and the High Priest of the Temple at Jerusalem appointed not by the Jews but by Rome. Jesus was their common enemy, a dangerous rabble-rouser. Within one to three years [he had] managed to become enough of a public threat that he had to be eliminated.'

Khoren Arisian, New York Society for Ethical Culture

30

The land where Jesus lived was part of the Roman Empire. The Romans were an occupying power who used their army to put down any opposition. They allowed the Jewish people some control over their own affairs. There was a Jewish council called the Sanhedrin, made up of chief priests and scribes. However, the Jewish people mostly resented living under occupation – with soldiers on the streets, taxes being due to a foreign ruler, and a general feeling of oppression. Jesus often taught about how the Jewish people should relate to the occupying power.

Jesus was brought up as a Jewish boy. His family took care to keep the *Torah* – the 'Teaching' in the first five books of the Jewish Bible, which contain the commandments that Jews must live by. Until he was thirty, Jesus lived in the village of Nazareth in Galilee. He began work there as a carpenter. A turning-point in his life was when he was baptised by his cousin John in the River Jordan. The Gospels record that

Jesus heard the voice of God saying 'You are my own dear son. I am pleased with you', and from then on understood what work he had to do.

Jesus then spent three years as a travelling preacher and healer. He soon attracted a following, as he became known as a charismatic preacher. His parables and sermons spoke to people's hearts. His message was also revolutionary, at times completely opposite to traditional Jewish ideas of his time.

The Jewish religion in those days was organised and ruled over by the chief priests in the Temple at Jerusalem. The chief priests divided people into those who were ritually pure and could therefore take part in worship at the Temple and those who were ritually impure and therefore could not take part in the worship. The priests had great power, prestige, and knowledge of the *Torah*, to decide who was and who was not pure.

At times Jesus' lifestyle and teaching contradicted what the chief priests said. He mixed with people whom the priests counted as 'impure', such as tax collectors, lepers, and prostitutes. One Gospel story tells that Jesus allowed a prostitute to wash his feet with her hair, and then told her that her sins were forgiven (Luke 7: 36-50).

◀ *Jesus' baptism by John is described in Mark 1: 9-11.*

1 **a** What do you learn from these two pages, about the person of Jesus?

b Jesus has been described as a rebel, rabble rouser, public threat, and charismatic preacher. Justify any two of these claims, using material from this unit.

c In what ways would the Jewish religious authorities consider Jesus a threat?

In what ways was Jesus' teaching revolutionary?

Jesus challenged people to rethink their whole way of seeing the world. The central theme of his teaching was the Kingdom of God, by which he meant the rule of God. Jesus told people to accept God as their king and to put God at the centre of their lives. He taught his followers what this means in practice. He taught that, when you put God first, your values and priorities change in a dramatic way.

A summary of Jesus' main teachings is found in a sermon he preached in Galilee, known as the Sermon on the Mount. This sermon has been called Jesus' manifesto of the Kingdom. The new social order of God's kingdom is contrasted with the legal and social order of Jesus' day. Some extracts are quoted here [B -H].

2 Choose one teaching from the Sermon on the Mount – maybe the one that presents the greatest challenge for you. Try living out this teaching for a week. Keep a diary to record your thoughts and actions. Report back to the class on what happened and whether you think Jesus' teaching is practical or unrealistic.

source B

Thoughts are as important as actions

'You're familiar with the command "Do not murder." I'm telling you that anyone who is so much as angry with a brother or sister is guilty of murder.'

Matthew 5: 21-22

source C

Doing good, God's way

'Be especially careful when you are trying to be good so that you don't make a performance out of it. It might be good theatre, but the God who made you won't be applauding. When you do something for someone else, don't call attention to yourself … When you help someone out, don't think about how it looks. Just do it – quietly and unobtrusively. That is the way your God, who conceived you in love, working behind the scenes, helps you out.'

Matthew 6: 1-4

source D

Loving others

'Here's another old saying that deserves a second look: "Eye for eye, tooth for tooth." Is that going to get us anywhere? Here's what I propose: "Don't hit back at all." … No more tit-for-tat stuff. Live generously.'

Matthew 5: 38-42

'You're familiar with the old written law, "Love your friend," and its unwritten companion, "Hate your enemy." I'm challenging that. I'm telling you to love your enemies. Let them bring out the best in you, not the worst.'

Matthew 5: 43-48

source E

Jesus' followers are like salt and light

'Let me tell you why you are here. You're here to be salt-seasoning that brings out the God-flavours of this earth. If you lose your saltiness, how will people taste godliness? Here's another way to put it: You're here to be light, bringing out the God-colours in the world.'

Matthew 5: 13-14

◄ *Jesus taught in many places around the Sea of Galilee. In the foreground of this picture is the Mount of the Beatitudes, where Jesus gave his famous sermon.*

source F

Do as you would be done by

'Here's a simple, rule-of-thumb guide for behaviour: Ask yourself what you want people to do for you, then grab the initiative and do it for them.'

Matthew 7: 12

source G

Priorities, money, and fashion

'Don't hoard treasure down here where it gets eaten by moths and corroded by rust or — worse! — stolen by burglars. Stockpile treasure in heaven, where it's safe from moth and rust and burglars … You can't worship two gods at once … You can't worship God and Money both.'

Matthew 6: 19-24

source H

Not worrying about surface things

'All this time and money wasted on fashion — do you think it makes that much difference? Instead of looking at the fashions, walk out into the fields and look at the wild flowers. They never primp or shop, but have you ever seen colour and design quite like it? The ten best-dressed men and women in the country look shabby alongside them.'

Matthew 6: 28-29

3 Imagine that you are working for Jesus' public relations and marketing office. Your job is to design a Power Point presentation to market the advantages of the Kingdom of God. You should consider:

– some of the main teachings;

– how the world would be better if people carried out Jesus' teachings;

– the challenges people will face in trying to live out Jesus' message.

The Beatitudes

The opening part of the Sermon on the Mount is known as the Beatitudes. Here, Jesus described the people who are especially close to God, or 'blessed' [I]. He was saying that these are the people who belong to God's Kingdom.

Think of how a mirror image is the opposite way round from the object it is reflecting; and of how the negative of a photograph shows dark areas as light. When he listed the qualities of those who would be blessed, Jesus was presenting a mirror image, or negative, of his actual world – the opposite of the way things really were. The priests were outraged, for they believed that they were especially close to God.

The priests' lives were based around officiating at the Temple. They oversaw the ritual purity of Temple worship. But Jesus was praising another kind of purity – inner purity of heart. The priests would have felt that Jesus was undermining their importance as mediators between people and God.

One way of viewing Jesus is as a mouthpiece of God, speaking out against injustice. In this he can be likened to the Jewish prophets, such as Amos and Jeremiah, who called people to live in a more moral way and to show compassion for others. Jesus cared passionately that society should be just and compassionate. He taught that God cares about all human suffering and its causes and he called people to stand on the side of the poor and the oppressed. One could make a good case to say that Jesus was killed because he stood against the powers of his day and encouraged people to follow his vision of a different social order. Many people have been inspired by this alternative vision to spend their life serving others.

➤ *Some people go out of their way to help those less fortunate than themselves. Others ignore them (opposite). Do you agree with the Pope that many people today live by 'the modern world's beatitudes', which are the reverse of Jesus' teachings?*

> **source 1**
>
> ### The Beatitudes (Blessings)
>
> Blessed are the poor in spirit
>
> Blessed are they that mourn
>
> Blessed are the meek
>
> Blessed are those who hunger after righteousness
>
> Blessed are the merciful
>
> Blessed are the pure in heart
>
> Blessed are the peacemakers
>
> Blessed are the persecuted
>
> *Matthew 5: 1-10*

4 a What does the word 'beatitude' mean? What other words could you use to replace 'beatitude'?

b How do Jesus' beatitudes [I] differ from the beatitudes of the modern world [J]?

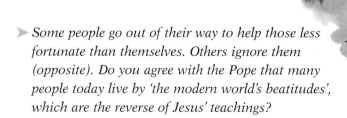

34

Pope warns against new Beatitudes of modern life

In March 2000, the head of the Catholic Church, the Pope, visited the place where Jesus gave his famous sermon. 80,000 young people gathered to hear the Pope speak. He encouraged them to become 'courageous apostles' of Jesus' teachings and he said that the Beatitudes, together with the Ten Commandments, offer 'a roadmap for the Christian life'.

He said that, to many, it seemed strange that Jesus had said 'Blessed are the meek, the persecuted and the poor in spirit', because he seemed to be saying 'Blessed are the losers'.

The Pope said it was hard for young people to accept such teachings when in today's world it is so often the proud and violent, the unscrupulous, and the devious who seem to prosper.

He described what seem to be the modern world's beatitudes:

'Blessed are the proud
Blessed are the violent
Blessed are those who prosper at any cost
Blessed are the unscrupulous
Blessed are the pitiless
Blessed are the devious
Blessed are those who fight
Blessed are the persecutors
Yes says the voice of evil,
They are the ones who win.
Happy are they!'

5 In a book entitled *Jesus rules OK*, the writer Frank Cooke said: 'The Sermon on the Mount is dynamite. It is the most revolutionary of documents.'

  a What do you think he means? Do you agree with his assessment, based on the Beatitudes?

  b What do you think the political and religious authorities of Jesus' time would have thought?

What did Jesus' miracles prove?

The Gospels give a clear impression that one reason why many ordinary people followed Jesus was that they believed he could work miracles. Jesus soon became known as a healer and miracle worker, as well as a preacher. The Gospels include over 100 cases in which Jesus is reported to have healed people or driven out evil spirits from inside them. In a world without modern medicine, Jesus the healer was bound to draw big crowds.

▼ *This picture from a church in Athens, Greece, shows Jesus healing ten lepers (Luke 17: 11-19).*

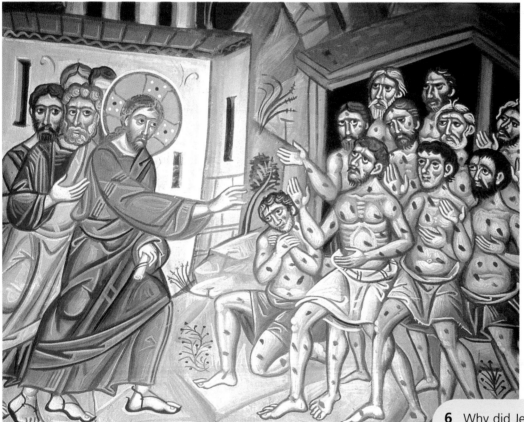

When Jesus healed the sick, he did more than make them better; he brought them back into respectable society. In Jesus' time, people believed that sickness was a punishment from God for sins that the person or their family had committed. By healing them Jesus brought them back into a relationship with God; they were no longer impure and so they could play a full part in Temple worship.

Like Jesus' teaching, the miracles of healing brought Jesus into confrontation with the chief priests. They said that Jesus was undermining their authority and the whole religious establishment of the day. Jesus was becoming a serious threat.

6 Why did Jesus heal people? What do you think was the purpose of his healing miracles?

7 Explain why the religious authorities felt threatened by Jesus. Make sure you refer to both his teaching and his healing.

Some people describe miracles as occasions when God crosses over from eternity into human time and brings about what cannot be caused in any other way. Christians believe that miracles did not end when Jesus died. Many people still experience God's power in their lives [K].

The Church continues Jesus' healing work in several ways. Christians are involved in medical treatment and research. They are involved in taking relief to the poor and hungry and in bringing about justice. And there is also a ministry of healing, in which people are supernaturally healed from illness [L].

source L

In its first report on healing for 40 years, the Church of England calls for healing to be an important part of the ministry of each parish church. 'It is … an integral part of the ministry, which should be to preach the gospel and to heal the sick,' commented Dominic Walker, the Bishop of Reading. 'We need to be educating every parish and looking at how a responsible healing ministry can be worked out throughout the Church.'

source K

A modern miracle

An amazing event on Christmas Day, 1972, had a profound effect on Catholics who lived in poverty on the rubbish dumps in Juarez, Mexico. Father Rick Thomas took seriously what Jesus said when he fed 5,000 people from a few loaves of bread and fish [Mark 6: 30-44]. Father Rick had invited the poor to gather for Christmas dinner. With his team, he had prepared 125 meals – but about 350 people turned up. Father Rick said a prayer to God and distributed the food. When it was given out, the food did not end. Even when the people had eaten all that they could, there was enough food left over to give to three orphanages. People believed that God had performed a miracle like the feeding of the five thousand.

Some Christians understand Jesus' miracles in a symbolic way. For example, there is an account of Jesus calming a storm on the Sea of Galilee (Matthew 8: 23-27; Mark 4: 35-41; Luke 8: 22-25). Whilst some Christians believe that Jesus showed miraculous power over nature by calming the wind and waves, other Christians think that the stormy sea in the story stands for the upsets and troubles people experience in life. The peace Jesus brings is an inner peace and security.

8 a Read the Bible account of the miracle of the feeding of the five thousand (Mark 6: 30-44). What similarities do you notice between this account and the account in source K?

b What do you think would have been the effect of the miracle in source K on the people who benefited from it? What do you think their understanding of it would be?

2.3

In what ways is Jesus' death important today?

The religious authorities felt threatened by Jesus' revolutionary teaching and acts of healing. They had to do something to protect themselves. The only way forward seemed to be to get rid of Jesus.

Jesus' death on a cross has become the defining image of Christianity. In any church you are likely to find more than one cross – perhaps a cross with Jesus nailed to it, drawing attention to his suffering; or an empty cross, drawing attention to the belief that Jesus was raised from the dead. Christians remember Jesus' suffering and Resurrection in particular at Easter. The 'Resurrection' is the word used for Jesus' coming to life again.

1 Watch two video versions of the Easter story and see how they differ. Which version did you prefer? Explain why. Give at least three ways in which the versions are (a) different and (b) similar?

2 Read two Gospel accounts of the Easter story (e.g. Mark and Luke). Then (a) produce a story board for one version; (b) create a table to list the similarities and differences between the two accounts.

▲ *Christian pilgrims in Jerusalem raise a cross during a Good Friday procession.*

38

During the week before Easter, called 'Holy Week', Christians think about all the events leading up to Jesus' death [A].

source A

The events of Holy Week

Jesus travels to Jerusalem with his disciples for the Jewish festival of Passover. He stays with Lazarus, in Bethany, a two-mile walk away.

'*Palm Sunday*': Jesus enters Jerusalem and crowds greet him as a king. This unnerves the Roman authorities, anxious about disturbances in the city during festival time.

Monday: Jesus goes into the Temple and shows his opposition to the chief priests by driving out the merchants selling animals to be sacrificed for Passover. The priests make a massive profit from trading in these sacrifices, so Jesus is undermining their power base. He says: 'You have turned the Temple into a hideout for thieves!'

Jesus speaks out openly, predicting the destruction of the Temple and, by implication, the end of the chief priests' control of religious matters [Luke 21: 5-6]. Jesus goes on to predict the end of the chief priests' rule when he tells the parable of the tenants in the vineyard [Luke 20: 9-16]. It is as if Jesus is provoking the religious authorities to action.

As Luke's account comments, the chief priests and teachers of the Law are afraid of the people and have been trying to find a way of putting Jesus to death secretly [Luke 22: 2]. As the Jewish authorities do not have the power to sentence people to death, they need to recommend to the Roman Governor that there are political reasons for condemning Jesus. Therefore, they accuse Jesus of (a) telling people not to pay taxes to the Roman emperor, (b) claiming to be a rival king, and (c) trying to cause a riot.

Thursday: Jesus celebrates the Passover meal with his disciples. After supper he takes his closest disciples with him to pray in the quiet Garden of Gethsemane. It is here that the Roman authorities arrest him. He stands trial and is sentenced to death on a cross, as a common criminal.

On the Friday of Holy Week, Roman soldiers led Jesus through the streets of Jerusalem to be crucified at a place called 'The Skull'. It is thought that the place of crucifixion was a quarry outside the city walls. At 9am, Jesus was nailed to the cross with the mocking words 'King of the Jews' placed above his head. By 3pm he was dead.

Many churches have a series of paintings or sculptures, called the 'Stations of the Cross', which represent stages on Jesus' journey through the streets of Jerusalem to his death. Christians use these 'Stations' to retell the Easter story and also to relive it – so that they bring the past into the present. Christians sometimes design their own 'Stations' to represent the suffering of people today.

➤ *The 11th Station of the Cross outside a church in Majorca.*

Artists have represented Jesus' death and Resurrection in many different ways. In the two paintings here, Matthias Grünewald and Otto Dix both draw attention to the belief that Jesus joins people in their suffering.

➤ *This is a panel from the Isenheim Altarpiece painted by Grünewald in 1512-15. It was made for a hospital caring for victims of the plague. Patients would meditate on Jesus' suffering, likening it to their own. Jesus joins the sufferers and shares their pain.*

▼ *In 1929 the German painter Otto Dix wanted to remind people of the pain of the First World War. He used Grünewald's design but turned the figures into soldiers riddled with bullets and dead in the trenches. In the right wing of this triptych there is a figure of compassion lifting a wounded soldier.*

Dix's painting is a crucifixion without Jesus. It shows the suffering not of one man but of all humanity in war. It raises similar questions to all paintings of the suffering of Jesus on the cross: How have I contributed to his suffering? What is my response when I see suffering? Am I willing to give compassion and help to those who suffer?

Stigmata

The word 'stigmata' refers to marks that appear on a person's hands, feet, or side, resembling the wounds that Jesus suffered when he was nailed to the cross. Since Jesus' death a number of people, called stigmatics, have experienced these marks on their bodies. The stigmata appear, blood pours from them for a time, and then, in most cases, the stigmata just as suddenly disappear and heal. Sometimes marks also appear on a stigmatic's head, as if made by a crown of thorns. As well as the marks, some stigmatics participate in a vision of the whole trial and crucifixion of Jesus. All these experiences are felt to come from God.

The first recorded stigmatic was Saint Francis of Assisi, who experienced his hands and feet being pierced with nails while he was praying in 1224. Since then there have been over 300 recorded stigmatics. One of the most famous was Padre Pio [B, page 42]. It is alleged that there are 18 stigmatics alive today.

5 Suggest why most stigmata appear on people on Friday or during Easter.

3 Imagine seeing Grünewald's painting on holiday, and writing a postcard home describing its features. What would you draw attention to? How would you describe the hands, face, body, legs, and feet? What do you think the plague victims would have felt as they looked at this painting?

4 In Dix's painting, pick out the upturned figure of the soldier riddled with bullets. Which of the figures in Grünewald's painting do you think he represents? How has he been painted?

An account of the time says that St Francis prayed that he might feel Jesus' sufferings. Then 'streams of fire and blood' from Jesus' wounds pierced his hands, feet, and heart.

The case of Padre Pio

Padre Pio bore the wounds of Jesus on his hands, feet, and side for 50 years. He was born into a peasant family in southern Italy and became a Catholic monk and priest. He wrote that, on 20 September 1918, 'after I had celebrated Mass, I yielded to a drowsiness similar to a sweet sleep … I became aware that my hands, feet, and side were dripping blood. Imagine the agony I experienced and continue to experience almost every day. The heart wound bleeds continually, especially from Thursday evening until Saturday. Dear Father, I am dying of pain because of the wounds and the resulting embarrassment I feel in my soul. I am afraid I shall bleed to death if the Lord does not hear my heartfelt supplication to relieve me of this condition.'
(Letters 1, No. 511)

▲ Pilgrims crowd round a statue of Padre Pio in Messina, Sicily, southern Italy, in 2002.

The Roman Catholic Church acted swiftly. Photographs were taken and medical experts sent for. There were scabs, almost an inch across, on the back and front of Padre Pio's hands. Both feet were in a similar state. The chest stigmata, three inches long, gave the priest more pain than the other wounds, bleeding much more freely. Padre Pio reckoned that he lost up to a cupful of blood on some days. Only in his final days, in the late summer of 1968, did the stigmata diminish. He was buried in the monastery where he had lived all the 50 years since his stigmata first appeared. In that time the remote village had changed into a major pilgrimage centre.

Several explanations are given for the appearance of stigmata:

1. Stigmata are produced in a natural manner, as a result of a strong imagination of the sufferings of Jesus.

2. Stigmata are supernatural. In support of this, people point to the fact that doctors have not succeeded in curing the wounds. Futhermore, sometimes the wounds give out a sweet perfume.

3. Stigmata are the result of severe emotional stress. There is evidence that stress can cause marks to appear. For example, an American professor of psychology reports a wartime case of an officer who in the past had been tied to his bed by the wrists. Years later, during nightmares, he produced lines of blood where he had previously been tied.

6 What, if anything, do stigmata prove? Do you think they are a blessing or a curse?

7 Which of the explanations of stigmata do you find most convincing? Explain your choice, using the material in this section as evidence.

2.4

What does the Resurrection of Jesus mean for Christians today?

Jesus died on the cross and was buried on a Friday, but Christians believe that on the following Sunday he was raised back to life: this is called the Resurrection. The Gospels contain accounts of many people seeing Jesus after his Resurrection. Although there is no description of the Resurrection, three things convinced members of the Early Church that Jesus had risen from the dead: (1) the tomb in which Jesus had been buried was empty [A]; (2) Jesus appeared to people after his death; (3) they felt his presence among them.

▲ Pilgrims visit the tomb cut in the rock, where Jesus' body is said to have been placed. Jesus' burial is described in Luke 23: 50-56.

source A

MYSTERY AT THE TOMB

The body of Jesus of Nazareth, who some called King of the Jews, has disappeared from the tomb. Jesus was buried last Friday, before the Sabbath. This morning, when some women went to the tomb to anoint the body, they found that the stone in front of the tomb had been rolled away and the body was missing. Some believe that the body has been stolen.

1 a What do you think could have happened to Jesus' body? In small groups, make a list of suggestions to share with the rest of the class. You will need to consider the possible involvement of the following people and their reactions: the disciples, Roman soldiers, Jewish leaders, God.

b As a class, collect your solutions in the form of a table.

c Weigh up the claims of each solution. Which solution do you think is the most believable? Explain why.

2 If you lived in those times, how would you go about finding out what happened on that Sunday morning? Who would you want to interview? What questions would you ask them?

WHAT DIFFERENCE HAS JESUS MADE? 43

Life after death

The biblical book of Acts tells us that Jesus' resurrected body remained on earth for 40 days. After that, Jesus ascended – went up – to heaven to be with God the Father. This is the Bible's way of saying that Jesus is alive and continues to be present with people in a spiritual way.

Belief in Jesus' Resurrection is central to the Christian faith [B] and it is the foundation for the Christian belief in life after death: the belief that a person's life does not end with their physical death, but continues forever in a relationship with God. The Apostles' Creed, a Christian statement of belief, ends with the words: 'I believe ... in the resurrection of the body, and the life everlasting.'

source B

'Because Jesus rose from the dead I know that he is alive today. When I pray to him he listens and guides me.'

Musa

source C

On the cross Jesus spoke to one of the thieves crucified with him:

Thief: 'Remember me, Jesus, when you come as king.'

Jesus: 'I promise you that today, you will be in paradise with me.'

Luke 23: 42-43

source D

'Christ has been raised from the death, as the guarantee that those who sleep in death will also be raised.'

St Paul, 1 Corinthians 15: 20

source E

'There are many rooms in my Father's house, and I am going to prepare a place for you.'

Jesus in John 14: 2

source F

'I am the resurrection and the life: whoever believes in me will live, even though he dies.'

Jesus in John 11: 25

source G

St Paul describes resurrection

'Some sceptic is sure to ask, "Show me how resurrection works. Give me a diagram; draw me a picture" ... We do have a parallel experience in gardening. You plant a "dead" seed; soon there is a flourishing plant. You could never guess what a tomato would look like by looking at a tomato seed ... This image of planting a dead seed and raising a live plant is a mere sketch at best, but perhaps it will help in approaching the mystery of the resurrection body – but only if you keep in mind that when we're raised, we're raised for good, alive forever! The corpse that's planted is no beauty, but when it's raised, it's glorious ... the seed sown is natural; the seed grown is supernatural – same seed, same body, but what a difference from when it goes down in physical mortality to when it is raised up in spiritual immortality!'

1 Corinthians 15

3 a Use sources B-G to write a paragraph about the Christian belief in life after death.

   b The image of the transformation of a caterpillar through a chrysalis into a butterfly is sometimes used to explain the transformation that happens at resurrection. In small groups, write a story for young children using the idea of the caterpillar to explain the Christian belief in the resurrection of the dead.

Do you believe in life after death?

Here are some students' reactions to this question.

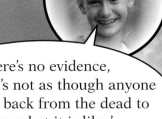

'There's no evidence, is there? It's not as though anyone has come back from the dead to tell us what it is like.'
(Katrina)

'People believe in life after death in order to comfort themselves. It's not real.'
(Anthony)

'Life on earth isn't fair – there has to be a way in which God can give justice, rewards, and punishments.'
(Sofia)

'I believe there's a life after death because all religions teach that death is not the end – all those millions of people can't be wrong.'
(Margaret)

'I believe in life after death because some people have had near-death experiences where they have glimpsed into the other world.'
(John)

'If there isn't a life after death, where do ghosts come from?'
(Anita)

4 a What reasons do the students give (a) in favour and (b) against belief in life after death?

b Which of the statements is closest to your view? Explain why.

5 a In small groups, survey opinions about life after death from people you know (parents, friends, and members of a faith community). Plan your questions carefully. Organise the responses in the form of a table. You could use a spreadsheet to record, present, and analyse the data you receive.

b In what ways have the responses you have received helped you to clarify your own thoughts?

c Which of the responses were 'religious' and which were 'not religious'?

d Discuss the reasons why there can be no 'right' answers to the questions you have asked, only beliefs.

6 Choose or develop five sayings or quotations that express your own thoughts, questions, or reactions to the issue of life after death.

7 a Imagine that you are going to meet the 'creator' of the universe. In groups, brainstorm questions that you would like to put to this 'creator' or 'someone who knows everything'.

b Consider the ways Christians might answer these questions.

What is the significance of Jesus' Resurrection?

The Christian belief that Jesus rose from the dead is celebrated throughout the world during the festival of Easter. This is the most important Christian festival.

> ➤ *A common way of celebrating Easter is through the use of Easter eggs. They vary around the world: in the UK they are often made of chocolate, in Russia of wood or porcelain, and in Eastern Europe they are dyed real eggs. The egg represents new life. It is a symbol of joy and happiness. Russian Orthodox Christians may give each other Easter eggs painted with an Easter scene.*

Before he died, Jesus had said to his disciples: 'Lo, I am with you always, even unto the end of the world.' (Matthew 28: 20). Jesus was promising that he would not abandon his disciples – he would be with them whatever happened. Since the Resurrection, Christians have believed that although Jesus is physically absent, he is spiritually present among them. This belief gives Christians hope, especially at difficult times. Here are some ideas about what the Resurrection means to Christians today.

● By raising Jesus from the dead, God showed that He has power over death.

● Jesus' Resurrection gives people hope, since they can believe that there is life after death for them also.

● The Resurrection shows that suffering and death are not the end. Suffering can be transformed [H].

● Jesus' Resurrection shows that Jesus is present with people today.

● 'Resurrection' is a quality of life that people can experience on earth.

8 **a** Find out how Easter is celebrated around the world. The following website is useful: http://cgi.cnn.com/ EVENTS/world_of_faith/ 9604/07/easter.gallery/

b Identify and explain some symbols of new life found in these celebrations.

Paintings of the Resurrection

9 a The Resurrection is one of the most difficult things for artists to paint. Why do you think this is?

b In the painting on this page, how does Grünewald express the Resurrection? Which parts of the biblical story does he represent? Which symbols does he use? Do you think he is successful?

Grünewald painted this picture of the Resurrection to console the patients in the plague hospital (see page 40). The stone lid of the tomb is cast aside and the sleeping guards are scattered as if by an explosion in the night. Jesus' trailing gown changes colour as it floats up with him, turning first to red like a royal robe and finally to gold. Jesus' body is no longer torn, although the five wounds on his hands, feet, and side are still there. These wounds give out rays of golden light and Jesus' face shines like the sun.

➤ *This panel from the Isenheim Altarpiece represents the Resurrection.*

source H

'Grünewald shows what nobody saw. He not only shows us the miracle of the resurrection. He compels us to see the significance of the resurrection. Unlike the women or apostles we need neither mourn nor doubt beside the empty tomb. We are made witnesses to the explosive triumph of light over darkness, and we realise that death and life will never be the same again.'

Neil MacGregor, in *Seeing Salvation – The Resurrection*

10 a Look at all of the pictures of the Resurrection on pages 47-49. Describe what you like and dislike about each of them and explain why.

b Which of the paintings do you think captures best the Christian belief in resurrection? Explain why.

In 'Christ of Saint John of the Cross', by Salvador Dali, the Crucifixion hovers above Port Lligat in eastern Spain, where Dali lived and worked. He painted this in 1951, as a reflection on the atomic bomb dropped on Hiroshima on 6 August 1945. The painting shows a world over which the resurrected Christ keeps constant watch. As spectators, we belong to the calm world below, but the painting also gives us a view of both Christ and the world, as God the Father might see them.

In the painting on page 49, the British painter, Stanley Spencer, associates the Resurrection with the Last Judgement. This is when Christians believe Jesus will come again, at the end of historical time, to judge people. Spencer does not show Jesus as a threatening judge, but as a loving motherly figure who nurses two babies cosily in his arms. Spencer understood 'Resurrection' in two ways: first, as involving the raising of a person after death – as shown in the naked bodies being raised from the graves; and second, as the achievement of a state of perfect peace and love – which can come to anyone at any time and place on earth.

▲ *'Christ of St John of the Cross' by Salvador Dali, 1951.*

11 a What strikes you about Dali's painting? When you look at it, do you look down from the top, or up from below? Look at the proportions – how does the world appear? Why do you think Jesus is placed between the world and God? Why do you think Dali set his painting in Port Lligat in Spain?

b Look carefully at Jesus' hands. Who or what is holding Jesus to the cross?

Spencer explores the idea that resurrection is an experience that people can have here and now on earth. In Spencer's own life, although he experienced two failed marriages, much loneliness and illness, he was able to recognise 'resurrection moments' of joy and love. He believed such moments were promises of the ultimate love that people would experience when they were united with Christ in the afterlife.

12 Do you think it is OK for a painter to show Jesus as a mother figure? What do you think Spencer is trying to say?

13 a Make a list of the experiences of perfect peace and love shown in Spencer's painting.

b Have you ever felt a wonderful sense of perfect peace and love? Do you find such experiences easy or hard to describe?

14 Why do you think Spencer painted his Resurrection scene as though it were happening in the village in which he lived? Why did he put himself in the painting?

▼ *'The Resurrection, Cookham' by Stanley Spencer, 1924-27. Spencer was born in Cookham, Berkshire, and this was where he mainly lived and worked.*

How are people changed by belief in the Resurrection?

Jesus' Resurrection brought about dramatic changes in the lives of people who were close to him, such as his disciples Peter, James, and John. They had been so afraid when Jesus was arrested that they had run away and deserted him. After his crucifixion, the disciples were a frightened group, hiding away from the authorities. But after seeing the resurrected Jesus they were transformed into people willing to spread the 'good news', even if doing so brought them suffering and death. Many of Jesus' early followers were crucified, or stoned, or thrown to lions. The belief that Jesus had overcome death gave these early Christians hope when they were being persecuted.

Enemies of Jesus were also transformed. Probably the most dramatic example is that of Saul of Tarsus. He was the chief persecutor of Christians in the years after Jesus' death. But he had a life-changing encounter with the risen Jesus while he was on his way to Damascus (see Acts 9: 1-19). This changed him into becoming the greatest teacher of Jesus' message. He spent the rest of his life spreading the news about Jesus.

Belief in the Resurrection leads to action. Like the disciples and Saul, Christian believers through the centuries have been willing even to risk their own lives to spread their beliefs about Jesus. The Resurrection is about new life [I] and can also encourage people to transform social and political situations [J] in order to bring about new life.

➤ *Many people have dedicated their lives to spreading the Christian message, often braving torture and death. For example, one of Romania's most widely known Christian leaders, Richard Wurmbrand (1909-2001), spent 14 years in prison and was repeatedly tortured for running the church 'underground' during Communist rule of the country, when Christianity was banned.*

15 Complete a paragraph beginning: People are changed by belief in the Resurrection in the following ways.

16 **a** Write down all the words and phrases used in source I to talk about the Resurrection.

  b What do you think Dostoevsky means by Raskolnikov 'passing from one world to another'?

  c Raskolnikov was given a second chance. Think of an occasion when you were given a second chance. What did it feel like? In what ways could it be said to be 'a resurrection experience'?

The raising of Raskolnikov

Raskolnikov is a main character in the famous Russian novel, *Crime and Punishment*, by Dostoevsky. At the beginning, Raskolnikov is a student, who has fallen on hard times. He wants to commit a crime, and chooses to murder a money-grabbing pawnbroker. The novel describes how this act affects Raskolnikov, and shows how his guilt about the crime increases.

Another important character in the book is a young girl called Sonya. She has felt driven into prostitution in order to earn money to support her drunken father's wife and children and save the family from starving.

Sonya shows Raskolnikov a love he has not seen before. When he comes to confess his crime to her, she reads him the Bible story of Jesus raising Lazarus from the dead [John 11: 1-44]. This introduces the subject of resurrection. Raskolnikov must die to his old way of life, and therefore to his crime, and be raised a new man. Sonya persuades Raskolnikov to give himself up to the police.

Through hearing the story of the raising of Lazarus, Raskolnikov understands that he can start again, and is given a new life. The God who raised Lazarus from the dead has the power to raise Raskolnikov from the death of his sin, to lead a new life of hope.

Dostoevsky believed that, in each person, good and evil are in constant conflict. So, Raskolnikov, a murderer, is also a person of great charity – and, at the death of Sonya's father, he gives the family money for the funeral.

The novel ends with Raskolnikov facing his prison sentence with Sonya's support. In the last scene, he asks himself: 'Can her convictions not be mine now?' Dostoevsky ends: 'But that is the beginning of a new story – the story of the gradual renewal of a man, the story of his regeneration, of him passing from one world into another.'

Resurrection means action

'If we say we believe in the resurrection, the claim only has meaning if we believe in the possibility of transformed lives, transformed attitudes and transformed societies. The payoff comes in the action that accompanies the belief ...

There are two resurrections, but only one is available to us. The first is the originating event, the big bang that ignited the Christian movement. The second is the effectual resurrection which is the continuing impact of Jesus upon history. So resurrection happens when Rosa Parks in Montgomery, Alabama, decides she has had enough and refuses to go to the back of the bus. This was the beginning of the famous bus boycott that changed American history [see page 21 of this book]. In resurrection language, a whole people walked out of the tomb of *segregation* because a woman had the courage to refuse to go to the back of the bus. That was a resurrection moment. Resurrection is the refusal to be imprisoned any longer by history and its long hatreds. It's the decision to take the first step out of the tomb.'

Bishop Richard Holloway, *Doubts and Loves: What is left of Christianity*

17 a What does it mean to say that belief in the Resurrection is an action statement [J]?

b How could you, as a school, bring about transformation and resurrection in your local community?

18 Carry out your own research on why Christians believe Jesus' Resurrection is important. Use the knowledge and understanding you have gained from this unit to prepare a list of questions you could ask a visiting Christian.

Unit 3

What difference do sacred places make?

In this unit you will explore what makes certain places special and sacred and what effects these places have on religious believers. You will consider why people make special journeys, called pilgrimages, to these sacred places. Lastly, you will examine how the city of Jerusalem is sacred to three major religions, and how this has resulted in a struggle over its ownership for thousands of years.

▲ *Until 1950, the Potala Palace, high in the mountains, was the home of the religious and spiritual leader of the Tibetans, the Dalai Lama. 'Potala' means the home of the bodhisattva Avalokiteshvara (see page 17).*

3.1

What makes a place sacred?

Most of us need a special place where we can be on our own. It could be a room, or a place like the tree at the bottom of the garden or a quiet spot in the local park. It is a place to go and 'be ourselves'. We often like to put our stamp on our special places. In the case of a bedroom, we make it feel ours by putting up posters and decorating it with objects that mean something to us.

1 Do you have a special place? What makes it special? Are there particular times when you go to this place?

2 How have you made your own place special? What objects have you brought into it? What do these objects mean to you? Bring one such object into class and explain why it is special – perhaps for its historical or sentimental importance.

In the beliefs of many cultures, mountains are the living places of the spirits or gods. Mountains were seen as links to the sky, stars, and heavens. People have heard God speak to them on mountains. Here, pilgrims walk on Mount Sinai, where God is said to have spoken to Moses and given him the Ten Commandments.

3 Why do you think mountains have been a place where people feel that God has come close to them?

The religions of the world have special places, where people go to concentrate on spiritual things and where they feel particularly close to God. Some of these places are part of nature, such as caves, mountains, springs, and waterfalls. Others are human-made, such as pyramids, stone rings, temples, mosques, and churches.

4 Why do you think people built the earliest religious buildings – like the pyramids – to look like mountains?

Places that are special in this religious sense are called 'holy' or 'sacred'. They are set apart. Some holy places are shrines – places that are associated with a sacred person or object or an important religious event.

5 Imagine that you have visited one of the sites on this page. Write a postcard home explaining your feelings about it.

> Church steeples and towers can be seen as reaching up to a world beyond everyday reality. St Basil's Russian Orthodox Cathedral in Moscow was built in 1555-61. Many great shrines like this took hundreds or thousands of craftsmen many years to create. Many represent the greatest art creations of human civilisation.

6 If you were to create your own sacred space, what would it look like? Think about the atmosphere you would want to create, and the colours and objects you would use. What rules, if any, would you make to govern the place?

What effect do sacred places have on people?

Ancient legends and modern reports tell of extraordinary things happening at sacred places. Some people have been healed; others have had visions of saints or enlightened beings [A, B, C]. Many people say that visiting a sacred site has given their life a new sense of meaning and purpose. Often people feel that visiting the site brings them in touch with a spiritual or divine reality.

In many great sacred places, religious ceremonies have been performed for a thousand years or more. Throughout the day and night, priests and visitors sing sacred songs. In one Buddhist temple in Japan, priests have maintained an unbroken chant for 24 hours a day since the mid-ninth century. Martin Gray is a researcher who spent 16 years visiting over 1000 sacred sites in 50 countries. He believes that 'the spiritual power deriving from those ceremonies has continued to accumulate at the sacred places.' Because of the large number of people praying and meditating there, a place seems to become charged with feelings of inner peace and religious devotion. Just as a fire radiates warmth, or a magnet is surrounded by a magnetic field, so a holy place seems to give out, or be surrounded by, peace and holiness.

▲ *People show reverence at shrines by lighting candles. Why do you think that even today, when electricity is readily available, people still use candles to light these sacred places? What atmosphere does using candles create?*

➤ *Some people say that a sacred site is surrounded by an invisible 'field' of spiritual energy, which is like the 'force field' around a magnet.*

1 Have you ever entered a room and 'felt' the atmosphere? It could be a calm, happy, or even creepy atmosphere. What was it like?

2 Do you think that the practice of religious activities at sacred places gives them a spiritual power? Give reasons in your answer.

3 What does it mean to say that a sacred place is like a magnet?

If people know that miracles have occurred at a sacred site, they are confident that miracles could occur again and in their own lives. So stories and beliefs about miracles have a powerful effect on people.

4 a What does source A tell you about Ivanka's beliefs?

b Ivanka is a Roman Catholic. What evidence is there of this in the text?

c What questions would you like to ask Ivanka? What answers do you think she would give?

source A

On 24 June 1981, the Virgin Mary, Mother of Jesus, appeared in a vision to six young people in the mountain village of Medjugorje in Bosnia-Herzegovina. She has appeared there every day since then, at 5.40 pm. Each vision lasts three to four minutes. Mary gives messages to guide people to a closer relationship with God. 'Dear Children', Mary pleads, 'pray for peace, fast on bread and water regularly, and go to confession once a month. Be pure in your hearts and minds. Drive hatred out of your hearts and love one another.' Christians travel thousands of miles to witness these visions and there have been reports of miracles taking place there.

Ivanka, one of the six young people, explained: 'The first time, [as] Mirjana and I were ... returning to the village I happened to look toward the hill – and I saw a figure of the Madonna [Mary], bright and shining. I said to Mirjana: "Look, the Madonna!" Mirjana dismissed what I said with a wave of her hand, as if I'd been joking, and she said: "It's not very likely that the Madonna would appear to us." So we continued to walk toward the village. Mirjana did not even look where I pointed. When we got to Milka's house, Milka said: "Help me get the sheep and bring them home." So we turned around and started walking back to the fields. This time, all three of us saw the Madonna. We knelt down and prayed; then we got the sheep and chased them home. Later, Vicka and Ivan and the other Ivan joined us. [Today] I speak with Her normally, the same as I'm speaking now. Also, I hear Her voice and words in the normal way, as well as what the others say.'

▲ Pilgrims at Medjugorje.

source B

One visitor describes the effect Medjugorje had on her: 'I wasn't even a practising Catholic at the time. Then I went up the mountain. It was like a slap in the face. My faith returned right there. I went back to Ireland, but I couldn't get this place out of my system.'

The Times Magazine, 24 February 1996

source C

Scientific tests in 1984 concluded: 'No scientific discipline is able to explain these phenomena. We would be willing to define them as a state of active, intense prayer ... a state of contemplation with a separate person whom they alone can see, hear and touch.'

The Times Magazine, 24 February 1996

3.3

Why do people go on pilgrimage?

1 Think of a special journey you have been on – it might be a school or family trip. Why did you go? How did you prepare for the journey? Why was the journey special? Did you bring anything back?

Each day people make journeys and every journey is carried out for a reason. One special type of journey is called a pilgrimage. This is a journey to a site that is holy in the religion of the traveller. A person on pilgrimage is called a pilgrim. People go on pilgrimage for a number of reasons, including to seek physical healing or spiritual help or to find answers to difficult personal questions.

Many shrines have developed around places associated with a holy person, or around their tombs or relics. This practice is especially common in Buddhism, Christianity, and Islam. Pilgrims believe that the holy person remains spiritually in and around the relics and tombs. Sometimes the skeletons and bones are believed to have power to heal and answer prayers.

▲ *Christian pilgrims walk on their knees at the shrine of the Virgin of Guadeloupe, the patron saint of Mexico, in Mexico City. Why do you think these pilgrims are walking on their knees? How do you think it makes these pilgrims feel?*

source A

'England's Nazareth'

The shrine of Walsingham, in the small town of Little Walsingham in Norfolk, is one of England's most visited places of pilgrimage. The Walsingham story began in 1061 when Richeldis de Faverches, a pious lady of the manor, had a vision of the Virgin Mary, who showed her the house in Nazareth where the child Jesus was brought up. She was told to build a replica of the house in Walsingham, and she did so. But Richeldis did not know exactly where to build the house. Soon after it had been built, everyone was astonished to find that the wooden structure had moved about 200 feet, by mysterious forces. Miracles began to be associated with the simple little building and it wasn't long before pilgrims were flocking to 'England's Nazareth', as Walsingham became known.

2 It can take months or even years to reach a pilgrimage site, because walking is the traditional way for pilgrims to travel. Why do you think walking is the traditional method? What dangers and hazards would pilgrims face on their travels?

56

Muslims go on pilgrimage to Makkah, as we will see in Unit 3.4. While they are there they may also visit the tomb of the Prophet Muhammad in Madinah (see source B). Some Muslims who have made the pilgrimage or 'Hajj' paint scenes of it, afterwards, on the walls of their houses.

source B

Visiting the tomb of the Prophet Muhammad

'After the early dawn prayer, I visited the resting place of our Messenger. Standing in front of the Messenger is an experience that is unparalleled; there wasn't a dry eye in sight. It was the moment that everyone here had dreamt about. Everyone was involved in their own private discourse.'

Hajj Diary by Rafaqat Ali

3 What does this pilgrim mean when she says that 'Everyone was involved in their own private discourse?'

➤ Many Buddhists go to India, to visit places associated with the life of the Buddha. Bodh Gaya is the most famous pilgrimage site for Buddhists. It is here, under a bodhi tree, that the Buddha was enlightened. Today a descendant of that bodhi tree grows in its place.

As pilgrims go on a physical journey to a sacred place, so they also go on an inward journey, into their heart and soul. On a pilgrimage, the journey itself is often thought to be as important as the destination. Pilgrims have probably been told stories about the place and heard of miracles or visions that have occurred there. They have probably seen pictures and maps of the place. All these intensify their expectations of the sacred place. For many people, visiting a sacred site fulfils an ambition of a lifetime. Going to a pilgrimage site is like entering another world, a spiritual world, with different things to see, smell, touch, and hear.

4 What do you think it means to say that pilgrimage is 'prayer in action'?

source C

The Maha Kumbh Mela Festival

Every 12 years, crowds of Hindu pilgrims travel to Allahabad on the river Ganges, for the Maha Kumbh Mela, or Great Pitcher Festival. The story behind this festival is that long ago, the gods, led by Lord Indra, were about to lose a great war against the demon king Bali. Lord Vishnu, who preserves the universe, advised Indra to churn the great sea, in order to obtain the liquid of immortality, so that he would not die. When the pitcher or jug (the *kumbh*) of liquid came out of the sea, Indra's son, Jayanta, was changed into a bird and flew off to take the jug to heaven, where the gods lived. On the way, he was chased by demons and spilt some of the liquid at four places – Nasik, Ujjain, Hardwar, and Allahabad, making them holy. Jayanta's flight took 12 days, or 12 human years.

source D

'We were determined to acquire immortality by taking a dip in the Ganges. By dipping in the holy Ganges at Allahabad we not only wash away our sins but also earn blessings equal to a million holy acts.'

Rupa

▼ *Pilgrims at the Kumbh Mela Festival in Allahabad, January 2001.*

5 Thousands of Christian pilgrims go to see the plays at Oberammergau [E]. What do you think they hope to gain?

Pilgrims flock to holy places especially during festival times. However, religions also warn of the dangers of turning religion into a superstition by performing rituals at these sacred places and losing the real meaning of religion [F].

Oberammergau villagers rehearse for the Passion Play, about the suffering, death, and Resurrection of Jesus.

source E

The Oberammergau Passion Play

In 1633 the Austrian village of Oberammergau was a terrifying place. The smell of the Black Death hung in the air and every day people were dying. 84 people had died when the villagers met in the church. They made a bargain with God. They promised that, if God would save them from the plague, they would act out a play about Jesus' life and death every ten years. No further deaths occurred.

The villagers have kept their promise ever since. All the parts in the play are taken by people living in Oberammergau – almost half the 5,300 population are involved. One of them says 'Even businessmen come out with tears in their eyes. And they are people not used to weeping. You shouldn't underestimate the spiritual aspect. The place feels like a gasoline station where pilgrims come to fill up their spiritual tanks.'

source F

The founder of Sikhism, Guru Nanak, was born in India. At that time people believed that bathing in the river Ganges at certain holy places would wash away their sins. The Guru taught that mere bathing at these sacred places would not clean the mind; no lasting peace could be achieved without meditating on the Divine Name (the Nam):

'Shall we go to bathe at the
        pilgrim places?
No. Nam is the only true pilgrimage.
Pilgrimage is the contemplation
        on the Word
That gives inner spiritual light.'

Guru Granth Sahib, page 906

6 In what ways does going on pilgrimage show that a religious believer is committed to their religion?

7 Write a paragraph explaining why some people go on pilgrimage. Why do some religious teachers warn against rituals on pilgrimage?

8 Think of a time in your life EITHER when you have had to make a difficult decision OR when you have had to change your opinion. Write a private diary entry explaining your thoughts and feelings. What was the inner journey of the heart and mind like?

3.4

Why do Muslims go on pilgrimage to Makkah?

There is one hope that is shared by a fifth of humanity – the hope of going on pilgrimage to Makkah, the birthplace of Islam. This pilgrimage is called *Hajj*, which means 'visit to the revered place'. For all Muslims, going on Hajj at least once in their life is one of the five 'pillars' of Islam. It is a central religious duty [A].

▲ *This nineteenth-century print shows the cube-shaped building, called the Ka'aba, in the middle of the Grand Mosque in Makkah. The Ka'aba is the focal point of Islam. Muslims all over the world face towards it when they pray.*

source A

'Pilgrimage to the holy house is a duty laid upon people that they owe to God – those of them who can afford the journey to it. Those who repudiate it should remember that God is certainly independent of all creatures.'

Qur'an 3: 97

source B

The story of Makkah

- There is a tradition that the history of Makkah can be traced back to the beginning of human history. When Adam was expelled from Paradise, he came to the site of Makkah to build a temple in praise of God. Using stones from Mount Sinai (in Egypt), the Mount of Olives (in Jerusalem), and Mount Lebanon, Adam built the first Ka'aba ('House of God').

- Flood waters covered it in Noah's time and the area returned to desert.

- Later, Abraham (or Ibrahim, as he is called in Arabic) came to the place with his maidservant Hagar and their son Ishmael. He left them there, trusting them to the will of God, as he was aware that they did not have enough food or water to survive. Hagar tried desperately to find water, running seven times between Mount Marwa and the hill of Safa. Then she saw an angel, who asked why she was crying. When she answered, the angel touched the ground with the tip of a wing and a spring of water appeared, which was called Zamzam. Hagar and Ishmael lived well here.

- To test Abraham, Allah ordered him to sacrifice his beloved son Ishmael. Abraham took Ishmael to Mount Marwa and prepared to slaughter him. Allah was satisfied with Abraham's complete submission and replaced Ishmael with a sacrificial animal. It is in commemoration of this that animals are sacrificed during Hajj, and by Muslims all over the world at the festival of Eid-ul-Adha.

- Abraham and Ishmael rebuilt the Ka'aba on Adam's original site. Abraham put a sacred stone in the building. This stone was thought to be a heavenly symbol of humankind's soul, and it was beautifully white. As people sinned, the stone eventually became black. Today the stone is identified as a piece of meteorite.

- As well as building the Ka'aba, Abraham established the rituals of the Hajj. The rituals recall events or practices in the lives of Abraham, Hagar, and Ishmael.

- After many generations, the people of Makkah slipped back into paganism and put idols in the Ka'aba. They continued to hold a pilgrimage, but it became a season for festivities, alcohol, and vice. New rituals were introduced, such as circling the Ka'aba in the nude while clapping, singing, and whistling. The pilgrimage season was important for the people of Makkah, because it brought a lot of money to the city. This state of affairs continued for thousands of years.

- The Prophet Muhammad turned the people of Makkah away from idol worship, back to the worship of one God. At first, people did not want to return to the monotheism of Abraham and for 13 years they persecuted the Prophet Muhammad and his followers. The Prophet emigrated to Madinah and eventually his army conquered Makkah. They destroyed the idols and purified the Ka'aba.

- The Prophet Muhammad established the fifth pillar of Islam as a continuation of the pilgrimage to Makkah.

◀ *Every able-bodied Muslim who can afford it is required to make the pilgrimage called Hajj at least once during their lifetime.*

source C

'It's an amazing experience to be with millions of Muslim brothers and sisters all coming on the Hajj. I felt a great sense of brotherhood and unity. We came from all over the world.'

Everyone taking part in the Hajj must prepare themselves, in both mind and body.

'Before leaving for Makkah, we all had to make sure that our relationships with other people were right. We had to repay all our debts and put right any wrongs we had done.

When we arrived we spent a week being taught what was expected of us. Our heads were shaved as a form of purification and we all put on the seamless white garments called ihram, as a sign that we are all equal in the eyes of Allah. The ihram was worn by both Abraham and the Prophet Muhammad (pbuh). It is also a symbol of purity. It's a reminder to pilgrims to stop all quarrelling and not to have any sexual relations until after the end of the pilgrimage.'

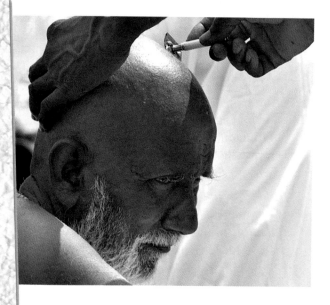

1

On the first day of Hajj, pilgrims perform the rituals of 'Tawaf' and 'Sa'y'. Tawaf means walking round the Ka'aba seven times. Sa'y ('the running', shown in this picture) means running seven times between Safa and Marwa. This is a reenactment of Hagar's search for water to quench Ishmael's thirst and the appearance of the sacred spring known as Zamzam. This water is now enclosed in a chamber in the Ka'aba.

2

Next the pilgrims go to Mina, an uninhabited village 5 miles east of Makkah. They stay overnight in Mina and then travel a further 10 miles to the plain of Arafat, to pray and meditate.

'Praying on Mount Arafat is a high point of the Hajj: a time when we think of the Day of Judgement. Many of us wept as we asked Allah for forgiveness for our sins. I felt especially close to Allah as I stood here. I felt as though I was on sacred ground. It is here that the Prophet Muhammad (pbuh) gave his last address. We left the plain feeling as though our sins had fallen away and we had a new start.'

3

'On the third day we moved to Mina where we threw pebbles at white pillars. We remembered the story of the Devil trying to persuade Abraham to ignore God's command to sacrifice his son. Throwing pebbles shows that we are trying to cast away all evil. By throwing seven pebbles at each pillar we show that we are willing to do this forever, since the number seven symbolises infinity.'

4

'After casting our pebbles we sacrificed a goat. Afterwards, the meat was given to the poor. By doing this we were remembering Abraham's willingness to sacrifice his son in obedience to God. It is a way of showing that we are also willing to obey God in all of our lives, as well as sharing our worldly goods with people less fortunate than ourselves.'

1 In what ways does going on pilgrimage to Makkah show that a Muslim is committed to Islam? Make sure that you comment on the preparation for the Hajj, the shaving of the head and the wearing of symbolic clothes, and the rituals that the pilgrims perform.

2 Explain how going on Hajj is a way of reliving the story of Ibrahim, Hagar, and Ishmael. How do rituals help Muslims to enter into this story? What lessons do Muslims learn by going on Hajj?

3 What is the religious significance of going on Hajj? What do you think a Muslim gains from carrying out this pilgrimage?

5

Pilgrims return from Mina to Makkah and perform the Tawaf again. As they do so, they may try to kiss or touch its sacred black stone.

'As we circled the Ka'aba we were reminded that all our activities must have God at the centre. It is amazing to see so many thousands perform this act. It really does make you feel that there is a oneness between God and humanity. In Arabic we repeated the prayer: "Lord God, from such a distant land I have come unto Thee ... Grant me shelter under Thy throne." We were all caught up in this whirling scene, caught up in our prayers to God and in harmony with all.'

3.5

Why is Jerusalem so special?

Every year thousands of pilgrims flock to Jerusalem to visit its religious sites. Jerusalem is holy to Jews, Christians, and Muslims. The Muslims even call the city *al-Quds*, which means 'the Holy One'. In this unit you will learn what makes this city different from other cities, and how it has a special place in the hearts of many religious people [A]. You will also learn how this religious passion has caused Jerusalem to be a city caught in conflict for much of its history.

Jewish Jerusalem

For Jews, Jerusalem is the ancient capital of the Jewish state and a direct link with their history. The city contains their most holy site – the Western Wall. This is the only remaining supporting wall of a platform on which the ancient Temple was built [B]. Several Jewish festivals are centred on the Western Wall. Many Jewish boys celebrate their Bar Mitzvah there. The Western Wall symbolises both the destruction of Jewish statehood, by the Romans, and the restoration of Jewish statehood in 1948.

1 Would it matter if archaeologists discovered that the Temple Mount was not the site of these key events [B]?

source A

'Visitors to Jerusalem are often on a kind of interior voyage ... Jerusalem is a city you visit in your mind or heart. It does not matter that the present Via Dolorosa with its stations of the cross is conclusively known to be a fairly recent tradition. It does not matter that the building now worshipped by the Jews as David's tomb and by the Christians as the Room of the Last Supper most probably dates from the later medieval period. These sites are defined by faith, not by science; they are sanctified by tradition and by centuries of uninterrupted devotion.'

Amos Elon, *Jerusalem City of Mirrors*

source B

'The Temple Mount is a specially holy place for Jews because it is here that Solomon's Temple stood. We believe that God's presence (which we call his *shekinah*) was especially felt in the Temple. Even though the Romans destroyed the Second Temple in 70 CE it has continued to be special to us as a symbol of God's presence on earth. The rabbis have taught that key events in God's relationship with humanity have happened at this spot. We therefore believe that this is the place where God created Adam and where Abraham offered up his son Isaac for sacrifice. It's not that all Jews actually believe in this in a historical way. But we do believe that Jerusalem is a symbol for God's presence and work in the world.'

Jacob Solomon, teacher

> *Praying at the Western Wall. People leave folded papers, scribbled full with prayers, in the gaps between the stones – in effect, making the Wall a 'mailbox to God'. Why do you think the papers are removed once a month by the caretakers of the Wall and ceremoniously buried in consecrated ground?*

2 a Why do Jewish people regard the Western Wall as holy? How does this affect their treatment of the Wall?

 b Read Psalm 48, which praises God's holy Temple. What impression of the Temple does it give you?

source C

'For two thousand years Jewish people prayed about Jerusalem and in the direction of Jerusalem. This happened even when there were virtually no Jews living in Jerusalem. It is because Jerusalem is the nerve centre of my faith. Here I feel a sense of belonging. My heart, soul, and whole being belong here. Anywhere else in the world is temporary, but Jerusalem is my permanent spiritual home. In Jerusalem I have a sense of final arrival by simply being here.'

Benjamin Boire, teacher

source D

'When I was growing up in the States, I learned about Israel and Jerusalem, like every other Jewish kid. While I knew it was a part of me, I had little interest in visiting. I made my first trip in 1987 at the age of 31. We landed on Wednesday afternoon and I knew by Saturday night that I had found my home.

I spent the next 13 summers working here, leading groups of teenagers through the Holy Land. I made *alliya* [took Israeli citizenship] in the summer of 1999 and to this day, I can't tell you why. My whole family lives in the States, my closest friends live there, and my income there was over 4 times what it is today. But there is something here in Jerusalem that tells me that this is the place for me. Even with all the problems that we are facing both within the Jewish people here and in dealing with our Palestinian neighbours, I feel more at peace walking the streets of Jerusalem than anywhere else in the world.'

Steve Toltz

3 What do sources B, C, and D tell you about the importance of Jerusalem, for Jews? Write your answer in the form of a reflective piece for your diary.

Christian Jerusalem

Jerusalem is sacred for Christians because Jesus spent the last days of his earthly life in the city. Many Christian pilgrims come to walk along the Via Dolorosa, 'the way of suffering'. It is said to be the route that Jesus took through Jerusalem on his way to be crucified. By re-living what Jesus went through, the pilgrims hope to find meaning in their own suffering.

The most sacred Christian shrine is the Church of the Holy Sepulchre [E]. It marks the traditional site of Jesus' death, burial, and Resurrection.

▲ *What do you think these pilgrims are feeling as they carry a cross along the Via Dolorosa?*

source E

'The site of Our Saviour's Crucifixion and Resurrection is the most sacred place on earth. Upon entering the shrine one's senses are overwhelmed with the sweet fragrance of roses and the scent of incense. Soft rays of sunlight from the golden roof play on the rough stone, creating mystical patterns which fuse into a stairway to Heaven.'

Nadya, Russian Orthodox Christian

Greek Orthodox Christians know the church as the Church of the Anastasis (Resurrection). They believe that each Easter God performs the miracle of lighting the Easter candle in the church by sending fire from heaven onto the tomb of Christ. The ceremony of the Holy Fire is thought to be a supernatural sign of the Resurrection that took place at this spot.

◀ *At the Holy Fire ceremony, light spreads outwards from the tomb at the centre as candles lit from the flame of the Easter candle are used to light the candles held by people nearby, and so on.*

4 Why is Jerusalem special to Christians?

5 Pick out the words that Nadya [E] uses to describe the atmosphere of the Holy Sepulchre. Is she using these words in a literal way? What do you think she is saying?

Muslim Jerusalem

For Muslims, Jerusalem is important because it is the place of the Prophet Muhammad's 'Night Journey' (Qur'an, 17:1) [F]. The Dome of the Rock is the third most sacred shrine in Islam.

◀ *Inside the golden-roofed Dome of the Rock, Muslims can see the rock from which they believe the Prophet Muhammad made his 'Night Journey'. The Dome of the Rock stands on the exact site where the Jewish temple used to stand.*

The rock over which the Dome of the Rock is built has significance for Jews, Christians, and Muslims. For all three religions, it is the legendary site from which God took the dust to create Adam, the first man. It is also said that Adam was buried there. It is the place where Cain and Abel offered their gift to God and where Noah built an altar after leaving the ark. It is the place where Abraham prepared to sacrifice his son Isaac (according to Jewish tradition) or Ishmael (according to Muslim tradition). In addition, in Islam, the rock is the place from which the Prophet Muhammad rose into heaven on his Night Journey. Visitors to the Dome of the Rock are shown his footprint in the rock.

6   Why is Jerusalem special to Muslims?

7   By using the sections on Jewish Jerusalem and Muslim Jerusalem, explain why conflict may exist between these two religions.

8   As a class, split into three groups. Each group should find out more about one of the three religions represented in Jerusalem. Use libraries and websites such as www.theresite.org.uk. Design a pilgrimage travel brochure for Jerusalem.

Conflict in Jerusalem

Jerusalem is so important to three religions that they have fought over the city for over three thousand years. Even as I write this book, sitting in my office in central Jerusalem, a violent conflict is taking place which has already killed over 1500 people in eighteen months. Both Israelis and Palestinians (Arabs from this land, which used to be called Palestine) claim historic and religious rights to rule over the city. The famous 'holy mount' in the middle of the Old City – the Jews call it Temple Mount, the Muslims call it Haram al-Sharif – is sometimes described as a likely trigger for the next world war. 'No other historic city evokes such inflammatory argument to this day,' says the Jewish Israeli writer Amos Elon.

The timeline below shows who has been in control of the city through the centuries.

An Israeli border policeman and a Palestinian confront each other as Palestinians were prevented from entering the Al-Aqsa Mosque in the Old City of Jerusalem for Friday prayers. The Israelis feared that fighting might break out in the Old City after the prayers.

9 Use the timeline to work out how many years Jews, Christians, and Muslims have each been in control of Jerusalem. What conclusions do you draw? How does this timeline explain why there is conflict in Jerusalem today?

1948 - present day State of Israel (Jewish)

1917 - 1948 CE British Mandate period (Christian)

3150 - 1006 BCE Canaanites

1006 - 586 BCE Israelites (Jewish)

586 - 37 BCE Persians and Hellenists (Greeks)

37 BCE - 324 CE Romans

324 - 638 CE Byzantines (Christian)

638 - 1099 CE Early Muslim conquests

1099 - 1187 CE Crusaders (Christian)

1187 - 1917 CE Mamelukes and Ottomans (Muslim)

68

The Golden Gate.

The end of the world

The city of Jerusalem is central to religious beliefs about what will happen at the end of the world [G].

- Some Jews believe that at the end of time the Messiah will proclaim the New Age from Jerusalem. The Messiah will enter Jerusalem through the Golden Gate. (This is the only gate in the city which is blocked.) Prominent Jews choose to be buried opposite this gate, because they believe they will be the first to be raised from death by the Messiah.

- Before his death Jesus told his disciples that he would return to earth a second time (John 14: 3). Some Christians believe that 'the Saviour will come from Zion [Jerusalem]' (Romans 11: 26) and will enter Jerusalem via the Golden Gate [G]. He will come to judge the earth.

- Muslims believe that at the end of time Allah will judge people. On the Haram al-Sharif there is a set of arches called the Arches of Judgement, where people will be judged.

source G

Web site looks for Second Coming

CHRISTIANS are being offered a 24-hour live Internet link to Jerusalem's Golden Gate so they can watch for the Second Coming from the comfort of their own homes.

A group of evangelicals in Hereford has set up a web site to monitor the Golden Gate via a fixed camera in the hope of recording the Messiah's return. The choice of the Golden Gate is based on a prophecy in the Old Testament Book of Ezekiel.

Christine Darg, who runs the Hereford Group, said: 'We believe Jesus could return close to the Millennium. Jews, Muslims and Christians believe He will enter Jerusalem through the gate that our "Messiahcam" is watching daily.'

Victoria Combe, *Daily Telegraph*, 18 May 1999

10 Do you believe that the world will come to an end? What do you imagine will happen?

11 What belief do the three religions share with regard to Jerusalem and the end of the world?

The Arches of Judgement.

What difference do sacred books and prayer make?

Unit 4 explores the importance of sacred books and prayer. For religious believers, reading or hearing the words of their sacred books and spending time in prayer are two ways in which they can communicate with God or be especially aware of the spiritual dimension of life.

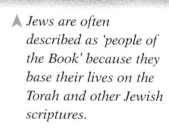

▲ *Jews are often described as 'people of the Book' because they base their lives on the Torah and other Jewish scriptures.*

4.1

What are sacred books?

Some sacred books are special because they contain the wisdom of the ages. They guide believers in how to live their lives. Some form the foundation of a religion. Some are believed to have been given by God, and to contain God's words and revelations.

Hinduism

Hindus have many sacred scriptures. A favourite is the *Bhagavad Gita*, often called the *Gita*. It was written between 200 BCE and 200 CE. It tells the story of Krishna, as an *avatar* (incarnation) of Vishnu, coming to earth in human form to teach people how to overcome evil and lead dutiful lives [A].

Judaism

The Jewish, or Hebrew, Bible is called the *Tenakh* and is made up of: (1) the *Torah* – the Law given to Moses on Mount Sinai; (2) the *Nevi'im* – the Prophets; and (3) *Ketuvim* – writings. Jews also have the *Talmud*, which is a collection of interpretations of the *Torah*, made by Jewish teachers. The *Talmud* is known as the 'Oral Torah'.

source A

'Our Holy book is the Gita, and if you read it ... you'll find the answer to all of your questions.'

Dr Gupta, quoted in
J. Bowker, *Worlds of Faith*

1 All the sacred books were written many years ago. Why do you think people still read them and follow their teachings? Do you think there is a need for a new sacred book for the twenty-first century? How would it differ? What would make it sacred?

Buddhism

The *Tripitaka* is the main collection of scriptures used by Theravada Buddhists. It consists of three sets of teachings of the Buddha, which some people say were written down in the second half of the first century BCE: (1) *Vinaya Pitaka* – rules for monks and nuns; (2) *Sutra Pitaka* – sayings and discourses of the Buddha; and (3) *Abhidharma Pitaka* – philosophical teachings. Mahayana Buddhists have a greater number of sacred texts.

Christianity

The Christian Bible, made up of the Old Testament and the New Testament, is the best-seller of all time [C]. Unit 4.2 looks at the Bible in more detail.

Islam

Muslims believe that their holy book, the Qur'an, contains the revelations made by Allah to the Prophet Muhammad [D]. They also read the *Hadith*, which are records of the sayings, actions, and life of the Prophet.

The Guru Granth Sahib is wrapped in beautiful cloths, and carried on the head, out of respect for the word of God that the book is believed to contain.

Sikhism

Sikhs believe that the Guru Granth Sahib contains the Divine Word (the *Gurbani*) which came to the Sikh Gurus direct from God. For this reason they treat the book with great reverence, as if it were a living Guru.

What influence does the Bible have?

1 Describe what is happening in this photograph. Why is the Bible being used in this way? What does it suggest about the authority the Bible has? Where do you think this authority comes from?

source A

'The Bible has authority. God inspired all the different writers of the Bible. Through the words of the Bible we learn what God is like. God speaks to us through the Bible. Some Christians believe that every word of the Bible is literally true. I do not, but I do believe that God speaks to me when I read the Bible. This is why I read the Bible daily because it tells me how I should live my life.'

Kathryn

➤ *When a British monarch is crowned, they are presented with a copy of the Bible, with the words: 'We present you with this book, the most valuable thing that this world affords. Here is wisdom. This is the royal law. These are the lively oracles of God.'*

source B

'It is impossible to rightly govern the world without God and the Bible.'

George Washington, 1732-99, the first US president

source C

'The Bible is no mere book, but a Living Creature, with a power that conquers all that oppose it.'

Napoleon Bonaparte, 1769-1821, French emperor

Many phrases and sayings used in the English language have their origin in the Bible. For example: an eye for an eye, and a tooth for a tooth (Exodus 21: 24); a man after one's own heart (1 Samuel 13: 14); escape by the skin of one's teeth (Job 19: 20); go from strength to strength (Psalm 84: 7); turn the other cheek (Matthew 5: 39); at the eleventh hour (Matthew 20); a good Samaritan (Luke 10).

2 To what extent has the Bible influenced our Western culture?

3 What do you think Gandhi meant, in source D?

4 What do you think the Chinese authorities saw in the Bible [E], which frightened them?

source D

'You Christians look after a document containing enough dynamite to blow all civilisation to pieces, turn the world upside down, and bring peace to a battle-torn planet. But you treat it as though it is nothing more than a piece of literature.'

Mahatma Gandhi

source E

CHINA RELEASES BIBLE SMUGGLER

A Hong Kong businessman, Mr Li Guangqiang, was recently sentenced to two years in prison for smuggling Bibles into China. He was accused of spreading 'an evil cult'. He was released from prison on health grounds. Mr Li is suffering from hepatitis B. However, he will remain under surveillance by the authorities.

February 2002

source F

A father was approached by his small son, who told him proudly, 'I know what the Bible means!'

His father smiled and replied, 'What do you mean, you "know" what the Bible means?'

The son replied, 'I do know!'

'OK,' said the father. 'So, son, what does the Bible mean?'

'That's easy, Daddy. It stands for "Basic Information Before Leaving Earth".'

From J. John and M. Stibbe, *A Box of Delights*

5 What basic information [F] does the Bible provide, necessary before leaving earth?

6 Compose your own 'sacred book'. You could include some or all of the following:
   • special letters you have received
   • favourite pieces of writing
   • special music, pop songs, hymns
   • diary extracts about important events in your life
   • quotations that have meant a lot to you
   • comments from friends, parents, and teachers.

With each item you include, give a brief explanation of why it is important to you and which part of your life it comes from.

4.3

What is prayer?

> **1** What do you think people are doing when they pray? As a class, brainstorm the word 'prayer'.

▲ *These boys took part in a prayer vigil, held a few days after the terrorist attacks on the USA of 11 September 2001.*

One of the most distinctively religious things that people do is to pray. Prayer is sometimes described in the following ways:

● It's a two-way relationship with a reality beyond oneself, which many people have called God [A, D].

● It's a conversation, involving listening as well as talking [B, C].

● It's a way of using your mind and body so that you are drawn into union with God [H, I].

● It's about trusting God [G].

Although prayer is often described as a conversation, this does not mean that it is easy [E]. Many people say it needs practice and self-discipline. It is for this reason that many people use set words and actions both to prepare for prayer and as they pray [F].

source A

'Prayer to me is when I feel that I want to open up to the experience of God. In other words, I can pray to him – more often than not when I've got problems; and it's strange to say, but somehow or other the answer's there, and it will come to me. It doesn't mean to say it comes within the first five minutes or anything like that, but somehow prayer is one answer, a way of getting some sort of response from yourself to God and from God to you.'

Christian, Ray Iles, quoted in
J. Bowker, *Worlds of Faith*

source B

'I call prayer a conversation, because I think any conversation is where there's two people, even if one is talking all the time and one is listening ... it's a conversation, in as much as I feel that God is listening ...

I do get something back. You're thinking about ... your life and your work, and your home; and you're saying to God, "Well, here it is; it may not be much, but here it is, and here I am: and I wonder what you think of it?"'

unnamed Christian, quoted in
J. Bowker, *Worlds of Faith*

source C

'Prayer is a conversation with my Creator, to remind me that I'm standing in front of my Creator, that I have a few days' life in this world, and that one day, today or tomorrow, I have to meet my God.'

Muslim, quoted in
J. Bowker, *Worlds of Faith*

74

'The purpose of prayer is to realise one's total dependence on God for every single aspect of one's life.'

unnamed Hasidic Jew, quoted in
J. Bowker, *Worlds of Faith*

'It is difficult ... to train your mind to cut off from thoughts entering your head while you're praying ... It takes years and years of practice to be able to cut off. But it does get easier as I get older.'

Jew, Mr Oliver, quoted in
J. Bowker, *Worlds of Faith*

2 What are people doing when they pray? Pick out phrases from the sources on pages 74–76 to illustrate your answer.

3 a If prayer is a conversation, how does God speak?

b What do you think it means to 'receive an answer to prayer'?

4 a What do you think St Francis [F] means when he prays 'Lord, *make us* instruments of your peace'?

b What is the main message of this prayer?

c How do you think saying this prayer sincerely will change the person who is praying? To what extent is prayer a form of action rather than only words?

▲ A Hindu woman prays by the river in Calcutta. Describe what is happening in the picture. How can you tell that something special is taking place?

A Christian prayer

Lord, make us instruments of your peace.
Where there is hatred, let us sow love,
where there is injury, pardon,
where there is doubt, faith,
where there is despair, hope,
where there is sadness, joy.

O Divine Master,
Grant that we may not so much seek
to be consoled, as to console,
to be understood, as to understand,
to be loved, as to love.

First it is in giving that we receive
it is in pardoning that we are pardoned,
it is in dying that we are born again,
to eternal life.

A prayer attributed to
St Francis of Assisi, 1182–1226

'This story is about a very great rabbi, and this rabbi could see that there was a terrible decree hanging over the Jewish people; and there was no way, through the prayers of all the people present, of breaking this decree, until one very simple man in the synagogue said, Well, let me try and see what I can do. He said, I can't read Hebrew, I can't put the words together, but I do know the letters of the alphabet. So the simple man just read out the letters of the alphabet; and he said to God – Here are all the letters of the alphabet: now you put them together into the proper prayer, and may my prayer be answered. And this prayer broke the decree which was hanging over the people.'

Jew, Mr Klein, quoted in
J. Bowker, *Worlds of Faith*

To help them concentrate, Hindus often recite the sacred sound 'Aum' over and over again [I] or repeat the name of a god, such as 'Hari-rama' or 'Hari-Krishna'. Muslims pray five times a day, following a set ritual. Christians, Muslims, and Hindus may use prayer beads. Each bead concentrates the mind on a particular prayer or, for Muslims, on one of the names of God.

source I

'Prayer for me is mostly the recitation of God's name over and over. It's like generating a connection with God, and it also gives you more control of your physical self by doing that. You can actually feel the connection. The Aum sound not only gives you control of your breath, but mentally it gives you that connection. I've never taken drugs, but I suppose, the way I've read about people taking drugs, when they feel sort of high, I suppose it's something like that. You feel like you're in heaven, that's the only way I can describe it.'

Hindu, Pranav Patel, quoted in
J. Bowker, *Worlds of Faith*

source H

'We have a pattern ... to each day. We get up in the morning and do our prayers; for me personally, it's a case of being thankful to God for the new day, and thankful that I am alive to be able to serve God for another day. For me, it's a routine; I have the bath and clean clothes and go in front of our gods and say whatever prayer is to be done.'

unnamed Hindu, quoted in
J. Bowker, *Worlds of Faith*

5 Do you have to be religious to pray? Why do you think non-religious people might pray?

6 Use the sources in this unit to help you make a list of why people pray.

What difference does prayer make?

What difference does prayer make to the person who is praying or to the person who is prayed for? Many people describe prayer as a conversation with God. How do they know that they are not just talking to themselves? Some people may have dramatic experiences in prayer [J], but this does not happen often. Some people say that, through prayer, they gradually become 'in tune' with how God wants them to be [K]. Some people say that they pray in order to bring about changes in themselves, to make themselves more loving. Other people say that, while they cannot explain what goes on in prayer, they know that something seems to happen [L].

source J

'My eldest daughter was quite ill ... For five days I stayed in hospital with her, and it was just through prayer, and knowing that I wasn't on my own, that I was able to cope with each day as it came. Prayer showed that there are two people who loved her and cared for her – which also made me feel better. I know Christ was working in her life ... Sister Charity [a nun] went in to see her and held her hand all day, and Gillian said later she felt a very warm glow, a very warm feeling; and she's never forgotten it. Only a few months ago, she said to me, "It wasn't just a warm feeling, Mum, it was a feeling of love ... that surrounded us."'

Christian, Jacqueline Rapson,
quoted in J. Bowker, *Worlds of Faith*

'Prayer is communion with God. You are talking to him. God says, "I am nearer to you than your jugular vein." He lives within us. In fact he says, "I dwell in your heart: your heart is my temple." And when we pray, we do dhikr [which] doesn't only mean saying, Allahu Allahu [O God, O God]; it means living it; living the qualities of God ... ArRahim, beneficent and merciful, is one of the [qualities] of Allah: that means that you must show compassion and beneficence to others.'

unnamed Muslim, quoted in
J. Bowker, *Worlds of Faith*

'There's been several times where your faith, I think, pulls you through ...

we've been really short of money... You've got to the stage where you've thought ... how on earth are you going to manage? Then all of a sudden someone gives you back the money that you lent them – on the very same day that you hadn't got any money. And you think, That's impossible: how did they know I didn't have any money? ...

You've run out of bread and someone says, 'Oh, I forgot to pay you back.' I've got one of those everlasting cupboards that people borrow things out of ... And it comes back in a measure that's so precise, the very thing you need is what's given back to you.

Christian, Mrs Iles, quoted in
J. Bowker, *Worlds of Faith*

---

7 Explain how praying makes a difference to people.

8 How much evidence is there in sources J to N that prayer works?

9 How reliable is source N? Does it prove that prayer works? What other information may you need to make up your mind?

10 If we wanted to discover whether prayer was effective, how could we find out? What evidence would you be looking for?

'I spoke with Jimmy Carter about the prayers he said during those tough negotiations at Camp David between Egypt's Anwar Sadat and Israel's Menachem Begin. I talked to David Crosby about his prayers while he was trying to stay away from drugs and alcohol. I spoke with Muhammad Ali about his prayers before he stepped into the boxing ring to fight Sonny Liston. In each case and in each story, these powerful and wellknown people asked for help. And this is where I started to learn about prayer. It's more than a conversation. It's more than a request for something to happen. Prayer is saying that you aren't running the show. It's saying you want to do the right thing. Prayer is more about who we are than what we want to do.'

Larry King, 'Praying with Fire', in *Olam Magazine*, special issue on Shabbat

RELIGION IS GOOD FOR THE HEART

Heart attack patients who are prayed for appear to recover faster than those who aren't. At the Mid-America Heart Institute in Kansas City, 500 patients admitted with heart attacks were allotted people to secretly pray for them. A further 500 were used as a control. Those in the prayed-for group had a significantly better recovery, being 11 per cent better off in terms of symptoms and test results. Patients and staff knew nothing about the trial, ruling out any placebo effect. The researchers suggest that thinking hard about someone in hospital with an attitude of prayer appears to be helpful.

Evening Standard, 23 November 1999

Unit 5

What difference do celebrations make?

In this unit you will think about how some of the world's religions celebrate key stages in human life, such as birth, becoming an adult, getting married, and death. You will see how ceremonies are a practical expression of religious beliefs, and you will evaluate what difference the ceremonies make to religious believers.

5.1

How should we celebrate the birth of a child?

What do Sikhs do when a baby is born?

Sikhs believe that each person has an immortal soul, which is reborn after death in another body, human or animal. The soul can become free from the cycle of death and rebirth and be joined with God – but this is only possible from life as a human. Therefore the birth of a human baby is an event to be celebrated.

Sikhs recite prayers of joy and thanks from the Guru Granth Sahib, and some families arrange for a reading of the whole of the Guru Granth Sahib. They take gifts, sometimes money, to the gurdwara, and may donate a silk cloth covering for the Guru Granth Sahib, called a *rumala*. To share their joy with the whole community, many families choose to supply the food for the community meal in the *langar*, the dining hall at the gurdwara.

Soon after the birth of a child, a naming ceremony is held, usually at the gurdwara. Family and friends are invited. The *granthi*, the person who reads the Guru Granth Sahib in the gurdwara, carefully opens the book at random. This is a way

▲ *A Sikh family bring their new baby to the gurdwara for a naming ceremony.*

1 a In small groups, discuss how people celebrate the birth of a baby. What would you do to celebrate the birth of a baby when or if you have children? Why do people want to mark the start of life in a special way? Share the responses of your group with the whole class.

b Why do you think religions mark the birth of a baby in a special way?

78

of leaving the choice of the reading to God. All teachings in the Guru Granth Sahib are thought to be equally relevant. The first letter of the first word at the top of the left-hand page is given to the parents, to be the first letter of the baby's name. The parents, and sometimes other members of the family, then discuss what name the baby should have [A].

Sikh names are chosen for their meaning. Most of the first names can be used for either sex, but all girls are given the second name Kaur, which means 'princess', and all boys are given the second name Singh, meaning 'lion'. This follows the teaching of Guru Gobind Singh that all people are equal.

At the end of the ceremony *Karah Parshad* ('holy food') is distributed to all present. It is a sweet mixture of sugar, water, butter, and semolina, brought and prepared by the family.

▼ *Sometimes the Sikh baby is given amrit – a nectar made of water and sugar crystals. The granthi dips the double-edged ritual sword, called the khanda, into the amrit and gently touches the baby's tongue with it. The remainder of the mixture is given to the mother to drink.*

source A

'Our first son was born in the UK. Having got the letter P from the Guru Granth Sahib, I chose Prubjoht. To make it easy for teachers and friends, my wife wanted his name to be Prithvi. Because my father, Jawala, died when I was young, we added Jawala so that our son would be able to remember his grandfather's name. Thus we gave a name for his birth certificate as: Prithvi Jawala Prubjoht Singh. This allows him to use any of the three first names on legal documents.'

Jaspal Singh Sindhar, from Sikhnet, Discussion Forum

source B

'People come to North America and completely change their names to fit in. For example, someone will say, "My name is Baljinder but you can call me Bill." I think that is totally wrong ... I go to a school in a town where I am the only Sikh person, and I wear a turban. My name is Harnarayan, and everybody calls me by that. A lot of people have said that I should have a nickname but I know that the name I have is the name God has given to me, and I am not going to let anyone change that. Sikhs have to take a stand. We should explain things, like why we wear turbans. Our Gurus have made our religion in such a way that we stand out in any crowd. We should respect that and follow our religion to its full extent.'

Harnarayan Singh, age 13, from Sikhnet, Discussion Forum

2 Why do Sikhs celebrate the birth of a child? Why do you think people share their joy with their local community?

3 What do you think about nicknames? What point is Harnarayan making in source B?

At a Christian baptism in a Greek Orthodox church, the priest immerses the baby in the water. In Roman Catholic and Church of England churches, the priest pours or sprinkles water over the baby's head.

What do Christians do when a baby is born?

Different Christian denominations have different services to mark the birth of a baby. Orthodox, Roman Catholic, Church of England, and Methodist churches have a service of infant baptism or christening. Baptist, Evangelical, and House churches have a dedication service. Both types of service welcome the baby as a new member of the Church.

Infant baptism

An infant baptism normally takes place at a Sunday church service. Through prayers and Bible passages, the parents and Church members express thanks for the birth of the baby. Then the parents present their baby for baptism. They make promises that they will help the child grow up to love and trust in God. Godparents, who are often friends or relatives of the family, also make promises to help bring up the child as a Christian and to fight against evil [C]. The parents and godparents gather around a font, a large basin of water. The priest sprinkles or pours water on the baby and the parents are given a lighted candle for their child.

source C

Promises to fight against evil

At a Church of England baptism, the priest asks the parents and godparents the following questions and they reply with the words in heavy type.

Do you reject the devil and all rebellion against God?

I reject them.

Do you renounce the deceit and corruption of evil?

I renounce them.

Do you repent of the sins that separate us from God and neighbour?

I repent of them.

Do you turn to Christ as Saviour?

I turn to Christ.

Do you submit to Christ as Lord?

I submit to Christ.

Do you come to Christ, the way, the truth and the life?

I come to Christ.

'The birth of Katie was a blessing straight from God. Each birth is a miracle, especially when you consider the formation of each brain, their little fingers and limbs. Because God has blessed me with Katie I wanted to acknowledge the fact that she is a gift from Him. I wanted to make a public statement and to promise to bring Katie up in a way that honours Him and gives Him the credit.'

Ellen Kingry

4 How do Christians show that the birth of a baby is a gift from God?

5 What reasons would a Christian give for wanting their child baptised? What does the baptism service mean to Christians? Why is water used in the service? What does the lighted candle symbolise?

6 Imagine that you are godparents. In small groups, discuss what you think being a godparent would mean in practice. Write a list of things that godparents should try to do.

7 Often parents ask for baptism for their baby because they think it is a nice celebration or because the grandparents want it. Do you think the Church should baptise children of parents who are not Christians?

◄ *In many churches a candle is lit and presented to the parents for their newly baptised baby. Some words are spoken, such as 'Shine as a light in the world to the glory of God the Father.'*

Dedication service

In a dedication service the parents bring their baby to the front of the church. They give prayers of thanks to God for the birth of the baby and make promises to bring up the child as a Christian [E, F]. As the child approaches adulthood, he or she may choose to take part in a 'Believer's baptism', to make his or her own Christian commitment.

source E

The introduction to a dedication service

'When parents wish to dedicate their children to the Lord, they are encouraged to make it known to us. It is the desire of this father and mother to bring their child to dedicate to the Lord. Proverbs 22: 6 says, "Train up a child in the way he should go, and when he is old he will not depart from it." Jesus said: "Let the children come to me, do not hinder them; for to such belongs the Kingdom of God".'

Promises at a dedication service

The parents are asked:

'Do you earnestly desire that your children shall grow up in the nurture and admonition of the Lord?

Do you commit yourself to dependence on the Lord to fulfil your parental duties?

Do you promise to pray for your children every day?

Do you recognise that it is primarily your responsibility to teach them the scriptures and to train them in the ways of the Lord?

Do you promise to so conduct your own life that your children may learn of Jesus and Christlike character by your example?

As a child's greatest need is to know Jesus, do you promise to speak of Him, to speak of personal faith in Him, and when your child reaches an age of spiritual understanding, to introduce him to your Lord and Saviour?

If this is your intention, please answer: "We do".'

Each godparent is asked:

'Do you promise to maintain close ties with the family and to lend a compassionate and listening heart to the parents and be present for the turning-points and milestones in the lives of these children? Do you promise to pray for this family, and without interfering, encourage this child to excel socially, academically and spiritually?

If this is your intention, please answer: "I do".'

8 Explain how and why the celebration of the birth of a child varies among Christian groups, using evidence and examples of different practices.

9 Consider the ways Sikhs and Christians mark the birth of a baby. What do the similarities and differences tell us about the two religions? Which religious practices do you find most interesting and why?

10 What's the difference between celebrating a baby's birth with a religious ceremony and celebrating it with a party?

'We saw the birth of our children as gifts from God. While they are our children to raise, they belong to God. Dedicating them at church was our way of acknowledging this publicly and before God. We didn't choose infant baptism as we believe that baptism is an individual's choice to follow God, and as our children become older it will be their decision to choose baptism or not.'

Debbie Denison

◄ *The Baptist Church is one denomination that has a dedication service for babies and a Believer's baptism for people who choose it. As for the first Christians, being baptised is a sign that they have accepted Jesus' teaching (Acts 2: 41). The person is lowered under the water and brought back up again. Read Romans 6: 3-4 to find out the meaning that this has.*

5.2

Grow up! – Becoming an adult

The period between childhood and adulthood is called the 'teenage years' or adolescence. It is a time of many changes, when you develop your own identity, apart from your parents. You make choices about your lifestyle and friends and dream of what you might be in the future. You may develop opinions, tastes, beliefs, and values that are different from those of your parents, and this can cause conflict [A]. In this unit, we will consider how religions mark the transition from childhood to adulthood.

▲ *How are these young people celebrating the coming of age of their friend? Is this a popular way of celebrating the move into adulthood? How else is it celebrated today?*

source A

Gabby asks for your advice

My mum and I don't get on well at all. We sometimes chat, but the conversation always ends in an argument, to do with school work or my friends.

My main problem is that she doesn't let me do anything that normal 12-year-olds do. She doesn't let me wear make-up, date boys, go out in the evenings with my friends, and when we go shopping, she doesn't like anything that I like.

Lately, this boy who I have fancied since the start of secondary school has asked me out and I don't know what to say. Should I say yes and completely ruin my relationship with my mum, or do I say no and regret it for ever?

UK law says that you can:

Get married with parents' agreement	at age 16
Buy tobacco	at age 16
Have sexual intercourse	at age 16
Learn to drive a car	at age 17
Vote in a government election	at age 18
Marry without any need for parents' consent	at age 18

1 a What are the differences between being a child and being a teenager?

b What arguments do teenagers have with their parents? Why do you think there is often conflict between parents and teenagers? What things do teenagers object to, and why?

c In what ways do teenagers want to be independent? When do you think they should be allowed to be independent?

2 a When do you think a teenager becomes an adult, responsible for their own actions? Do you think it is the same for boys and girls? Do all people grow up at the same time?

b In groups, write out a 'tick list' of things that show someone is an adult.

c How does UK law mark the beginning of adulthood? At what age does the young person take on new responsibilities?

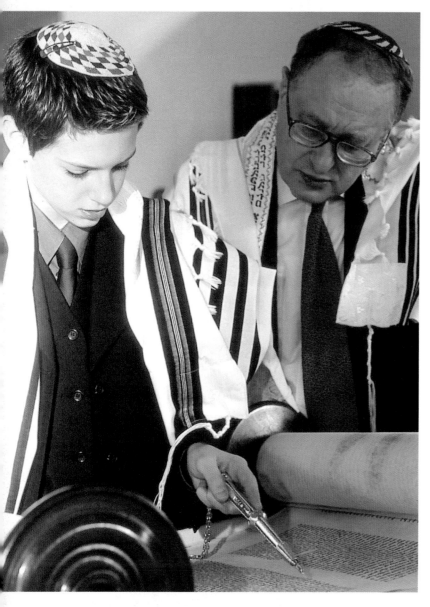

3 **a** Do you know how different religions celebrate the time when a child becomes an adult? Have you been to any of these celebrations and, if so, what were your impressions?

b In a family that follows a religion, parents often take their children to religious services. At what age should a child be allowed to choose for him/herself whether to attend a religious service? At what age do you think teenagers are old enough to take responsibility for their own religious or 'other' behaviour?

◄ *In preparation for his Bar Mitzvah ceremony a Jewish boy learns to read from the Torah scrolls. He is also taught to wear the tallit (prayer shawl) and tefillin. These small leather boxes containing the words of the Torah are worn by some Jewish males during weekday prayers.*

Wearing the tefillin on your head and on the arm nearest your heart is a reminder to think about and love God's teaching.

The Jewish coming of age

According to Jewish teaching, a boy is an adult at the age of thirteen and a girl at twelve. The boy or girl then takes responsibility for carrying out the *mitzvot* (commandments) as an independent individual. From this point a boy is known as *Bar Mitzvah* (son of the commandment) and a girl as *Bat Mitzvah* (daughter of the commandment). To prepare for their *Bar Mitzvah* or *Bat Mitzvah* ceremony, Jewish boys and girls are taught to read the Hebrew scriptures, and learn about Jewish history and culture.

The *Bar Mitzvah* ceremony normally takes place in the synagogue on the Saturday following the boy's

The number of tassels making up the fringe of the tallit are a reminder of the 613 mitzvot in the Torah.

thirteenth birthday. The boy is called to read in Hebrew from the Torah scrolls and after he has completed the reading his father says: 'Blessed is He who has released me from responsibility for this child.'

The *Bar Mitzvah* ceremony can be traced back as far as the thirteenth century, but it is only in the last one hundred years that many families have wanted to mark a girl's coming of age too. It is usual for a group of girls to study together and prepare for their *Bat Mitzvah* ceremony a year in advance. Jewish girls learn what it means to keep *kosher* and *Shabbat*. At the service after her twelfth birthday, in an Orthodox synagogue, the girl gives a short talk; but in a Progressive synagogue girls read from the scriptures in the same way as the boys.

4 **a** What two things does a Jewish boy learn about in the years leading up to his Bar Mitzvah? Why do you think these are so important to him?

   b When does a Jewish man wear his tallit and tefillin and why?

5 **a** Why do you think Bat Mitzvah is more recent than Bar Mitzvah?

   b What are the similarities and differences between the two ceremonies?

The Hindu Sacred Thread ceremony

The Hindu scriptures divide life into four stages, of which the first is the student or *Brahmacharya* stage. It is a time for learning, especially about the beliefs and practices of the Hindu religion. The Sacred Thread ceremony is a ritual which celebrates this stage of life and illustrates the responsibilities of being a student. The ceremony is called *Upanayana*, which means 'taking the child to the teacher'. In the past, it marked the time when a Hindu boy left home to study under a spiritual teacher or guru. Today, it is not necessary to leave home. The ceremony is regarded as a spiritual rebirth and afterwards, the boy is allowed to start studying the scriptures called the *Vedas*.

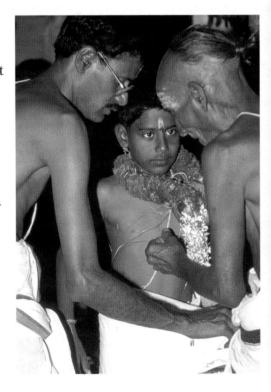

➤ *At the Sacred Thread ceremony, a thread knotted with three strands is hung diagonally across the boy's chest. He wears it throughout his life. The three threads represent the trinity of gods, Brahma, Vishnu, and Shiva.*

Taking Amrit – the Sikh coming of age

Many Sikhs approaching adulthood take part in a ceremony called *Amrit Chhakna*. This is the initiation ceremony that makes them members of the *Khalsa*, the community of committed Sikhs. It dates from the time of Guru Gobind Singh [C] and many parts of the ceremony [D] are modelled on his forming of the *Khalsa*. Each candidate makes promises, which affect the way they live their lives [E].

source D

The amrit ceremony

Anyone wishing to join the *Khalsa* must apply and be found worthy by five committed Sikhs, called *Khalsas*. They represent the *Panj Piare*. Sikhs can be considered for joining at any age, so long as they understand the vows that they will take.

Before the ceremony, which takes place in the gurdwara, candidates put on the five Ks. One of the *Khalsas* says a prayer and then there is a reading from the Guru Granth Sahib. The candidates stand and ask permission to join the *Khalsa*. One of the *Khalsas* explains the rules and obligations this involves.

Then the *amrit* is prepared. A steel bowl is filled with water, and sugar crystals are added. All the *Khalsas* stir the water with a double-edged sword, while hymns are recited. Then each candidate receives the *amrit* in the palms of their hands and it is also sprinkled into their eyes and onto their hair. This signifies the purifying of body and soul – what a person sees, thinks, and does. Finally each drinks a little from the same bowl until it is empty. The ceremony ends with a prayer, a reading of the Guru Granth Sahib, and the distribution of *Karah Parshad* ('holy food').

source C

Guru Gobind Singh founds the Khalsa

On Baisakhi Day in 1699 over 20,000 Sikhs came to Anandpur to meet Guru Gobind Singh. He appeared holding a sword and asked for volunteers willing to give up their lives for the faith. There was silence. Eventually one Sikh stepped forward. Guru Gobind Singh took him inside a tent and soon came out holding the sword apparently dripping with blood. He asked for another Sikh. One by one, four more Sikhs stepped forward and were taken into the Guru's tent. Each time the Guru came out with blood on his sword. After the fifth time the Guru appeared at the opening of the tent with all five men standing alive. He called them the '*Panj Piare*', meaning 'the beloved five'.

The five were given nectar made from water and sugar crystals, while holy prayers were recited – and this became the ceremony for initiation into the Sikh community, the *Khalsa*. The Guru also asked the beloved five to give him the nectar, called *amrit*, so showing that all people are equal before God. The Guru had tested the Sikhs' courage and willingness to die for their faith. By joining the *Khalsa*, Sikhs show that they are united and willing to stand firm, even when persecuted.

6 What do sources C, D, and E tell you about the responsibilities Sikhs take on when they take amrit? Have you made any promises about the way you live your life? What influenced you in making these promises? Why do you think it is important for Sikhs to make these promises in a public ceremony?

7 How does the amrit ceremony reflect its historical background?

8 How would you like to celebrate becoming an adult? Invent your own ceremony with rituals.

source E

'Before taking amrit I used to smoke and occasionally drink alcohol. Now I have no alcohol nor tobacco. I also spend more time with my Sikh friends and less time with non-Sikh friends.'

5.3

Why get married?

Every year, about 300,000 couples in the UK choose to commit themselves to each other in marriage for the rest of their lives. The government has promoted marriage as the basis of family life [A], but some say that this is going against the trend of modern society, where many people are choosing not to get married [B]. More couples are choosing to live together without getting married [C]. Also, four in ten British marriages now end in divorce. Are these signs that marriage is becoming out of date?

➤ *This couple chose to have their wedding ceremony underwater, at a scuba-diving resort in Indonesia.*

source A

Children to get marriage lessons
Schools in England have been told that they must teach children from the age of seven about the importance of traditional marriage. The guidelines are part of the new National Curriculum published by the government.
9 September 1999

source B

Marriage out of fashion
Marriage is officially going out of fashion, according to the latest government statistics. Regional figures from the Office for National Statistics show the number of marriages taking place is decreasing, with more couples opting to live together. Figures show that among single men aged 20 to 24, 57.5 per 1,000 got married in 1988 compared with only 20.2 per 1,000 in 1998. Among single women the figure declined from 95.6 per 1,000 in 1988 to 39.6 per 1,000 in 1998. On average, a quarter of people in the UK aged 18 to 49 were living with someone but not married between 1994 and 1996.

source C

Which couples stay together?
A study published by the Institute for Social and Economic Research at the University of Essex shows that only 36 per cent of children born to unmarried parents who live together are still looked after by both parents by the time the children reach 16. This compares with a figure of 70 per cent for children born to parents who are married.
quoted in *The Times*, 'What's love got to do with it....', 2 December 2000

1 **a** What do you think about marriage?

 b What reasons might people have for getting married?

 c What reasons might people give for living together without getting married?

 d What do you think is the difference between living together and getting married?

2 Why do you think the government considers marriage to be so important?

Marriage ceremonies

Although marriage ceremonies differ across continents and religions, many include some of the same ingredients. In both Christianity and Sikhism, marriage is considered to be a sacrament, a union blessed by God that people should not break. The marriage rituals create a bond between the man and woman. Christians speak of the couple becoming 'one flesh'. Sikhs talk about the fusing of two souls in marriage, so that they become inseparable.

◄ At a church wedding service, rings are blessed and exchanged, as a sign of the vows taken. The ring symbolises everlasting love. After this the priest says: 'I therefore proclaim that they are husband and wife. That which God has joined, let no man divide.' The priest blesses the married couple.

Christian marriage

In the Christian tradition marriage is a gift of God. In a Christian marriage service, the priest says: 'Marriage is a gift of God in creation through which husband and wife may know the grace of God. It is given that as man and woman grow together in love and trust, they shall be united with one another in heart, body and mind, as Christ is united with his bride, the Church.'

Many churches hold marriage preparation classes for couples planning to marry. The classes give couples an opportunity to think through the meaning of the vows that they will be making to each other and to God, in front of the community.

During the wedding service the couple exchange promises 'to have and to hold from this day forward, for better, for worse, for richer, for poorer, in sickness and in health, to love and to cherish, till death us do part.'

The bridegroom says to the bride: 'I give you this ring as a sign of our marriage. With my body I honour you, all that I am I give to you, and all that I have I share with you, within the love of God, Father, Son and Holy Spirit.'

Where would you like to get married?

In the past, marriage ceremonies could only take place in church or in a register office. Now, many other places are licensed to hold marriage ceremonies. These comments were posted on a website investigating views on where people would like to be married.

'I think that allowing people to get married where they want to ... will make marriage both more popular and more meaningful to the couple making the vows.'

'Proper preparation for a life together will make a marriage, not some fancy, trendy location.'

'I wonder whether permitting this to happen is a comment on the fact that marriage is now seen exclusively in terms of personal fulfilment rather than as a public commitment and the framework for rearing children.'

'Why get married at all if it is a civil arrangement? Marriage is about having God join you together.'

3 What do you think a couple needs to know about each other before they think about getting married?

4 Do you think that people who are not practising Christians and who do not attend church should be allowed to marry in church?

5 Prepare a speech for a debate on the question: Are religious marriage ceremonies out of date?

Sikh marriage – Anand Karaj

Most Sikh marriages are 'assisted'. This means that the parents of one of the couple have introduced them in the first place. Even when a man and woman meet without such an introduction and wish to get married, their parents become much involved. However, a marriage cannot take place unless both the man and woman agree to it.

The Sikh marriage ceremony is called *Anand Karaj*, which means 'ceremony of joy'. It must take place where the Guru Granth Sahib is present, and so it usually takes place in a gurdwara. The bride and groom sit facing the Guru Granth Sahib. The *granthi* normally conducts the ceremony and starts by reminding the couple of the commitments they will make. The *granthi* reads the *Lavan*, a hymn of praise to God, celebrating the love of marriage.

6 What do you think are the reasons for assisted marriages? What qualities do you think Sikh parents are looking for in their future son or daughter-in-law? Do you think these qualities are different from the qualities young people look for themselves? What do you think might be the advantages and disadvantages of assisted marriages?

MATRIMONIALS

Sikh family well settled in UK invite correspondence for their 24-year-old daughter, 5 feet 7 inches height, slim-built, working as a supervisor-cum-training officer with reputable company. Has done 2nd year in BA Honours +. Boy should be gursikh wearing a turban and having beard. Parties from UK should apply.

Hello. I am a Sikh female living in Malaysia. 28 years. Personality: warm, bubbly and nice. Looks: really presentable, height 5 feet 5 inches, slim. Education: currently doing MBA. Looking for a Punjabi man age 28-34 years, presentable to look at, a professional, height: 5 feet 9 inches above, caste not an issue as long as a Sikh, a decent guy with both east and west values. Looking for someone to live my life with, to care and share. Basically looking for a friend and a companion. I would not mind settling abroad, preferably USA.

The *Lavan* has four verses and after each one, the couple walk around the Guru Granth Sahib, each holding one end of a scarf. The first circle they make around the Guru Granth Sahib is for a life of sharing and work. The second is for the bringing together of the bride and groom in a relationship of love that casts out fear. The third is for detachment from desires, possessions, and pride. And the fourth is for the peace of the union between husband and wife. Each time they return to their starting position, they bow to the Guru Granth Sahib to show that they accept the teaching in the verse. The couple are pronounced man and wife and are showered with flower petals. The ceremony ends with a reading from the Guru Granth Sahib and is followed by a sharing of *Karah Parshad* and a celebratory meal.

Sikhs believe that marriage is not just a social contract between two people but also a spiritual union. The love between the couple is compared to the love and longing of the human soul for God and this idea is present in many of the hymns sung during the ceremony. Because the marriage is spiritual, the *Rahit Maryada* (code of conduct) discourages marriages between Sikhs and non-Sikhs. However, in some parts of India, marriages between Sikhs and Hindus are common.

In Sikh belief, a husband and wife are completely equal. Their relationship should be based on love, respect, equality, humility, and faithfulness. Marriage should be for life, but divorce is not ruled out if there is a complete breakdown of a marriage.

▲ *The scarf held by the bride and groom is a symbol of the strong but soft bond that marriage creates between them.*

source F

'When husband and wife sit side by side why should we treat them as two? Outwardly separate, their bodies distinct, yet inwardly joined as one.'
Guru Granth Sahib, page 788

7 Compare the beliefs behind Christian and Sikh marriages. What similarities and differences do you notice?

8 'Marriages between people of different religions don't work.'
   a What reasons might people have for holding this view? Refer to the teachings of two religions in your answer. You may like to consider what would be the difficulties of marrying someone who does not share your faith, and the effects this might have on your children.
   b What reasons might people have for holding the opposite opinion?

5.4

An appointment with death

None of us can miss our appointment with death. For all people, rich, poor, and of every culture or faith, death is the one certainty of life. We will explore the difference that religion can make, by giving death meaning. We will find out how religions remember their dead, through rites and rituals, and what beliefs lie behind these rituals.

1 How do you feel when you lose something? Is there a difference between losing something and losing somebody? What does it feel like to say 'goodbye' to a close friend? Have you ever had to say goodbye to someone who is dying? What did it feel like? What did you say?

2 How do you picture life? One suggestion is that life is like a bus station or an airport departure lounge. In it you make yourself as comfortable as possible and strike up some good friendships, but it is foolish to treat it as permanent. All people have to move on, say goodbye, go on another journey. Do you think this is a helpful image to have of life?

I do not think that very small children should go to funerals. It will frighten them.

It's important to teach children about death, in school. If they know what happens about death, it takes the fear out of it. It's just a normal part of life.

I think it is gross to put make-up on dead bodies so that they look good for the funeral. People are trying to hide away from death when they do this.

Death provides a horizon to life. It gives life meaning because every day is important. If life went on for ever, it would lose meaning.

Why does news on television rarely show us dead bodies? Surely if there is a war going on, they should present the reality of it.

When you die, let your body be used for medical use for saving other lives.

It's hard for me to believe that one day I shan't be here.

I would be afraid of cremation for myself in case I felt anything.

I'm frightened of death as I cannot imagine myself not existing.

When I'm dead, I won't know – or will I?

3 a As a class brainstorm the word 'death'. What feelings, colours, and words do you associate with it?

b Why do you think some people fear death?

c Why do you think other people are not frightened at the thought of death?

4 a Pick out the opinion on this page that is closest to your own view.

b Pick out the most interesting opinion, and explain why you find it interesting.

How does the Buddhist community deal with death?

Buddhists believe that there are important lessons to be learnt from death, which can benefit the way we live this life. Some Buddhists speak of death as a teacher, friend, or counsellor [A]. If death is a teacher, what can it teach us?

The sight of a dead man was one of the signs that prompted Siddattha Gotama (who became the Buddha) to question worldly pleasures and seek true happiness. After his enlightenment, the Buddha taught that an important step towards such happiness was to accept that nothing lasts for ever [B]. The existence of death confirms this teaching, since no one can take anything with them past death. This helps us to keep things in perspective. Buddhist funerals are important occasions for reflecting on these teachings.

Buddhists believe that, when someone dies, the soul is reborn and can continue its journey towards *Nirvana*.

source A

'I lost my mother four months ago ... My heart was torn open, and I experienced my own humanity perhaps more than I ever have. Life has an urgency now, I feel compelled to enjoy others more fully, to be in the present as much as I can. I must be in this moment because I will never have this moment, with this person, again. Therefore, death can be a teacher, because it brings home to us life's temporality ... Death is all around us. We will die and people we love will die. Understood this way, the only sensible course of action seems to be to seek that state where death cannot follow: Nirvana, the state of being awake.'

Shirley Galloway, 'The Meaning of Death in Buddhism', www.cyberpat.com/shirlsite

◄ *The funeral and cremation of a Buddhist monk in Korea.*

source B

'Know the body
to be as transient as foam, a mirage ...
As a flash flood
can sweep away a sleeping village,
so death can destroy
those who only seek the flowers
of casual sensual pleasures.'

Dhammapada 46-47

5 Source B uses a number of similes to describe the impermanence of life. A simile is an expression that describes a person or thing as being like someone or something else. For example, the body is like foam. Create two other similes that Buddhists could use to describe the impermanence of life. Write these as car boot stickers and create a frieze for the classroom.

6 If death is a teacher, what does it teach? Use the sources A to D to make a list of all the lessons that death has taught people.

source C

'A person who correctly grasps the inevitability of death becomes more focused on religious practice, since he or she realises that death is inevitable, the time of death is uncertain, and so every moment counts.'

John Powers, *Introduction to Tibetan Buddhism*

source D

'Meditation on impermanence shows you that everything in the universe is a constant flux, a process of becoming. It changes your view of how you "exist". You experience yourself and the world as much freer, less predictable, more mysterious, even magical. You start to hold life very lightly. You begin to see that craving, trying to hold on to things to gain security from them, is a strategy doomed to failure from the start.'

Vessantara, in 'The Cremation Ground',
Friends of the Western Buddhist Order,
www.fwbo.org/articles

How does the Jewish community deal with death?

When a Jewish person dies, their body is washed and wrapped in plain white cloth. Jewish mourning customs help people to remember their dead and to cry about their loss. The funeral usually takes place very soon after the death, partly out of respect for the dead and partly to help the mourners grieve. Most Jews are buried, although some Progressive Jews choose cremation. When a Jewish person is buried, their prayer shawl (*tallit*), with its fringe removed, is put into the grave with them. This symbolises that the need to keep the commandments is over. The Hebrew name for a cemetery is 'house of life' or 'eternal house'. The words of the funeral help Jews to face the fact that the person has died and will not return, and also that life goes on for those who remain.

There are several stages for mourning, which help Jews cry and then make a gradual return to life. These stages are:

- *Shiva* (meaning seven) – the first week after the death. During this time the family meets to share memories and stories. They sit on low stools, as a sign of 'low' feelings. Mirrors are covered or turned around and prayers, called *kaddish*, are recited. Mourners do not go to school or work in this week.

- *Shloshim* – the 2nd to 4th weeks. For the first month after the death Jews do not shave or cut their hair. Also, they do not attend any parties.

- The rest of the year. Every day, for a year after the death, close members of the family recite the memorial prayer (the *kaddish*). It does not mention death at all, but praises God as the giver of life. On the anniversary of the death, close relatives light a memorial candle. Within the first year the gravestone is set. It is customary for people who visit the grave to place a small stone on it. This is because Abraham, the 'father of the Jews', is believed to have used a pebble to mark the spot where his wife Sarah was buried.

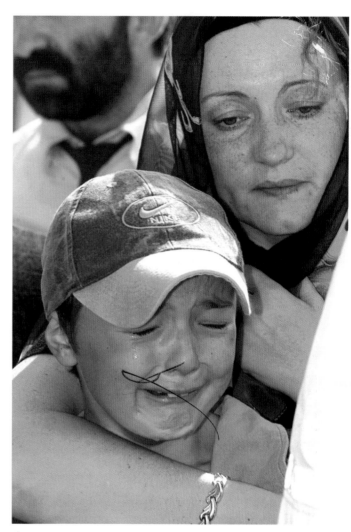

▲ *In what ways might Jewish mourning customs help a family after the death of a loved one?*

---

7 **a** What would you like to be remembered for?

b Why is every Jew who dies wrapped in a simple white cloth?

c Why do you think that Jews mourn for as long as a year? How do Jewish rituals help the mourners? Do you think it is helpful to spread the mourning process over a year?

8 At the end of this unit we should return to our key question and try to summarise what we have learnt in order to answer it: What difference do religions make to our understanding of death? Write your answer in the form of an argument.

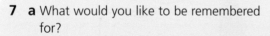

source E

'When we are dead, and people weep for us and grieve, let it be because we touched their lives with beauty and simplicity. Let it not be said that life was good to us, but, rather, that we were good to life.'

Jacob P. Rudin, American Reform Rabbi

Acknowledgements

Photographs

The Author and Publishers thank the following for permission to use the photographs in this book:

Art Directors and TRIP Photo Library: pages 4 (H. Rogers), 32-33 (H. Isachar), 35 (H. Isachar), 36 (H. Rogers), 39 (H. Rogers), 43 (H. Isachar), 46 (H. Rogers), 52 (B. Vikander), 53 bottom (Bob Turner), 54 (H. Rogers), 58 (Dinodia), 61, 62 bottom, 63 top, 65 (H. Isachar), 67 (H. Isachar), 69 top (H. Isachar), 72 top (H. Rogers), 82 (K. Cardwell), 83 (H. Rogers), 85 (F. Good);
Associated Press: pages 9, 42, 55;
Bridgeman Art Library: pages 40 top and 47 (Musée d'Unterlinden, Colmar, France);
Circa Photo Library: pages 30 top, 38, 69 bottom (William Holtby), 71 (John Smith), 79, 81 (John Fryer), 84 (Barrie Searle), 88 (John Smith);
Corbis Images: pages 6 (Peter Turnley), 7 (Richard T. Nowitz), 10-11 (Bill Ross), 15 (Chris Lisle), 17 bottom (Bass Museum of Art), 22 top (Bettmann), 23 (Flip Schulke), 24 (Pawel Libera), 25 top (Joseph Sohm; ChromoSohm Inc), 28 (© National Gallery Collection; by kind permission of the Trustees of the National Gallery, London), 31 (Werner H. Müller), 41 (Massimo Listri), 45 (Roy Morsch), 56 (Danny Lehman), 57 top (Otto Lang), 60 (Historical Picture Archive), 72 bottom (Bettmann), 76 (George H. H. Huey), 80 (Franz-Marc Frei), 92 (Nathan Benn);
Glasgow Museums: The St Mungo Museum of Religious Life and Art: page 48;
The Newark Museum/Art Resource, NY: page 27;
Christine Osborne Pictures: pages 53 top, 57 bottom, 62 centre, 63 bottom, 64, 66 top, 78, 90;
Staatliche Kunstsammlungen Dresden, Galerie Neue Meister: page 40 bottom;
© Tate, London, 2002: page 49;
The Voice of the Martyrs, http://www.persecution.com: page 50.

Quotations

The Author and Publishers are grateful for permission to reproduce the following copyright material.

Scriptures (pages 26, 27, 34 and 44, sources B, D, E, F) quoted from the *Good News Bible*, published by The Bible Societies/HarperCollins Publishers Ltd, UK, copyright © American Bible Society, 1966, 1971, 1976, 1992.

Extract (source C, page 44) from *The Dramatized Bible* edited by Michael Perry (Jubilate Hymns, 1989), copyright © Mrs B Perry/Jubilate Hymns, reprinted by permission of the publishers.

Extracts (pages 32, 33 and 44 source G) from *The Message* Bible by Eugene H Peterson, copyright © 1993, 1994, 1995, 1996, 2000, reprinted by permission of NavPress Publishing Group. All rights reserved.

Extract from *Thought for the Day*, BBC Radio 4, 23.2.02, reprinted by permission of the BBC and Professor Russell Stannard.

Extract from *Heart and Soul*, BBC1, reprinted by permission of the BBC and Tony Robinson c/o London Management.

Extracts from 'Paul's Letter to American Christians', 4.11.56, and 'I have a dream', 28.8.63, by Martin Luther King Jr, copyright 1963 Dr Martin Luther King Jr, copyright © renewed 1991 by Coretta Scott King, reprinted by arrangement with the Estate of Martin Luther King Jr, c/o Writers House as agent for the proprietor New York, NY.

Extract from 'Religion is good for the Heart', *Evening Standard*, 23.11.99, reprinted by permission of Atlantic Syndication.

Extract from article by Victoria Combe, *Daily Telegraph*, 18.5.99, copyright © Telegraph Group Limited 1999, reprinted by permission of The Telegraph Group Ltd.

Extracts from 'Visions on the Mount' by Anne McElvoy, *The Times Magazine*, 24.2.96, copyright © Times Newspapers Ltd, London, 1996, reprinted by permission of News International Syndication.

Extract from Stories of New Muslims by Helena, www.usc.edu/dept/MSA/newmuslims, 26 July 2002, reprinted by permission of the Muslim Students Association, University of Southern California.

Extracts from SikhNet Discussion Forum posted by Jaspal Singh Sindar and Harnarayan Singh, reprinted by permission of the authors and SikhNet.

Extracts from 'Out of this World' by Denis Prager and 'Praying with Fire' by Larry King, *OLAM Magazine*, special issue on the Shabbat.

Extracts from *Worlds of Faith* by J. Bowker (BBC, 1983), copyright © J. Bowker 1983, reprinted by permission of BBC Worldwide Ltd.

Extract from *Doubts and Loves: What is left of Christianity* by Bishop Richard Holloway (Canongate Books Ltd, Edinburgh, 2001), copyright © Richard Holloway 2001, reprinted by permission of the publishers.

Extracts from *One Minute Wisdom* by Anthony de Mello, SJ (Doubleday Image, 1985), copyright © 1985 by Anthony de Mello, SJ, reprinted by permission of Doubleday, a division of Random House, Inc. and the De Mello Spirituality Center.

Extracts (pages 15, 93) from *A Dhammapada for Contemplation* a rendering by Ajahn Munindo (River Publications) reprinted by permission of The Magga Bhavaka Trust.

Extract from *Christian Letters to a Post-Christian World* by Dorothy Sayers (Eerdmans, 1969), reprinted by permission of David Higham Associates.

Extract from 'The Milindapanha' in *The World of Buddha: an introduction to Buddhist Literature* by Lucien Stryk (Doubleday, 1968).

We have tried to trace and contact copyright holders before publication but have not been able to do so in every case. If notified, the publishers will be pleased to rectify any errors or omissions at the earliest opportunity.

Websites

Oxford University Press accepts no responsibility for material published on websites referred to in the book. Website addresses included were correct at time of going to press, but beware that these may change.

Index